APPRECIATION FOR *THE MISSING PEACE*

This book is a strong invitation to discover meditation as a liberating and life-giving dimension of the Christian life, as it is for those of many other religions.

Cardinal Timothy Radcliffe OP, author, former Master of the Dominican Order, Consultor to the Pontifical Council for Justice and Peace

This is a most remarkable book.

The author makes plain a wisdom tradition that has been largely hidden for centuries. With great clarity, the practice of contemplative meditation is demystified for the modern era. A sure guide on the path of transforming silence, this is a book to read slowly, to absorb, to live rather than analyse.

The Missing Peace invites us to clear a space in which to become aware of God's presence – and, in opening to this presence, to be opened to each other and the whole of creation. We come to know that all created beings are of one piece, created by the same Spirit, interrelated, and that nothing is separate.

We may feel powerless in the face of today's global adversities, believing there is little we can do to help. But as the author writes: 'When we are peaceful, even though we may well be unaware of it, we create small ripples of peace around us.' If we live the peace that lights the pages of this little book – the peace of God within – we will each bring sparks of this missing peace to the world.

Pauline Rudd, Professor Emeritus, University College Dublin, Founder Fellow of the International Society for Science and Religion

While we continue to see fewer and fewer people regularly attending church services, their deep, genuine longing for the depth-dimension of Christianity has only grown through the years. Sadly, most Christians have absolutely no idea that Christianity has anything to say about this, much less that it has its own vibrant contemplative tradition. This is largely due to the fact that it has never been presented to them.

The School of Contemplative Life will surely rate among the most significant responses to the spiritual longings of the people of this nation and abroad.

Through its debut book *The Missing Peace*, its growing online practice community and thoughtfully designed programme of retreats, the School will directly nourish and cultivate the depth-dimension of life, offering Christians – and seekers from all traditions – an accessible pathway to the wellspring of silence, compassion and peace flowing within.

Simply put, there is no other organization in the country quite like this, dedicated to helping people discover their groundless Ground, the eternal Mystery ever hidden with Christ in God.

Martin Laird OSA, Professor of early Christian studies at Villanova University, author of Into the Silent Land

This is indeed a valuable contribution to the literature on contemplation in the modern world.

Bernard McGinn, Professor Emeritus, University of Chicago Divinity School

To be a peacemaker means, first of all, becoming a person of contemplative prayer and active nonviolence. When the nonviolent Jesus calls us to be peacemakers, he invites us to be as nonviolent as him and like him, to spend intimate time each day with the God of peace that we might be disarmed to go forth into the world of war and spread God's peace through universal love and nonviolent action.

The Missing Peace offers beautiful, short reflections for the daily practice of contemplative peace which I intend to keep close by for those moments when I'm missing peace and struggling to stay nonviolent and loving. I hope everyone will take up these guidelines for the journey of contemplation, active nonviolence and Gospel peace-making, that together, we might all become peacemakers, the sons and daughters of the God of peace.

Revd John Dear, peace activist, nominated for the Nobel Peace prize by Desmond Tutu, director of The Beatitudes Center and author of The Gospel of Peace

Many years ago, one of the greatest discoveries in my life was that of silent prayer and being still. In a world of constant noise, distraction and conflict, *The Missing Peace* is an invitation to discover the treasure of silent prayer and enter more deeply into the mystery of God's love as we go on becoming who we are in relationship with God, neighbour, creation and with ourselves.

This book reflects the wisdom and insight of both ancient and contemporary teachers, with Jesus Christ at the heart.

This inspiring and beautiful book is not only deeply nourishing but is also extremely accessible and practical. With all that is taking place around us and within us, this book will be a good personal companion as the stories of our lives unfold.

The Rt Revd Rachel Treweek, Bishop of Gloucester and Anglican Bishop for HM Prisons

Chris Whittington is an engaging and trustworthy guide to the ancient contemplative tradition of the Christian Church; in this luminous collection based on a series of short talks, he shows his readers where to find the wells that contain the fresh spiritual waters for which so many in our culture thirst.

It is wisdom drawn from the Bible and from two millennia of practice; wisdom made accessible and practicable. Paradox abounds: what we most want is what we already have; the inner turmoil which disturbs and distracts us is in truth the gateway to blessings; the deepest desire of our hearts can only be come by if we let go of our desire for it.

Now more than ever, many of us are ready to study, ready to be taught, ready to learn together about how peace can knit us back together and renew our hope. Here we find out who God is and who we are; how to dive into the depths of our being, go exploring in the cave of our hearts, and find the treasure that is joy and peace.

Revd Dr Janet Williams, Vice Principal of St Hild College, author of Seeking the God Beyond: A Beginner's Guide to Christian Apophatic Spirituality

The short meditations found in this book are an elegant invitation to enter into meditative prayer. Each of them summons the soul afresh to encounter the living God.

In our hectic world and these uncertain times, the search for the divine Source of an indomitable and abiding peace may seem beyond our reach. This simple, unassuming guide, however, can help the receptive reader discover its presence within.

I heartily recommend this fine volume.

Addison Hodges Hart, author of The Ox-Herder and the Good Shepherd *and the Substack page, 'The Pragmatic Mystic'*

At the beginning of *The Missing Peace*, Chris Whittington quotes Thomas Merton:

> *In prayer we discover what we already have. You start from where you are, and you deepen what you already have, and you realize you are already there. We already have everything, but we don't know it and don't experience it. Everything has been given to us. All we need to do is experience what we already possess.*

This book does just that. It helps us discover what we have and shows us where to start and all that we, through prayer and contemplation, can recognize, deepen and become. Chris Whittington leads us with a simple clarity, wisdom and truthfulness. Drawing on writers of wisdom and his own experience this is a very valuable guide for all those who seek the life-giving path of the Spirit.

Revd Richard Carter, author of The City is My Monastery,
Priest at St Martin-in-the-Fields

Chris Whittington's new book, *The Missing Peace*, is a wonderful, timely and important contribution to the growing spiritual awakening in our time.

It is a particularly helpful and accessible resource in our journey of prayer and spiritual transformation. The structure of the book is beautifully organized. Chris simply and elegantly explores important theological, psychological and practical wisdom, insights and resources for our journey towards resting in interior silence and stillness.

The School of Contemplative Life is a wonderful growing practice community which meets twice weekly online with hundreds of people joining to learn, meditate and share together. The School is becoming a major spiritual oasis in our time.

I believe this book will significantly contribute to the restoration of Christian contemplative theological and psychological wisdom and practice for individuals and communities today.

The beauty, love, and joy of this essential teaching – its simple practice and path of interior stillness – shine through the book and the School, offering a way to personal transformation and to the healing of society and the world.

*Julienne McLean, psychologist and Jungian analyst,
author of* The Diamond Heart: Jungian psychology
and the Christian Mystical Tradition

ABOUT THE AUTHOR

Chris was introduced to meditation and the contemplative life when he went to live at the Benedictine monastery of Prinknash Abbey, England, where he spent time during many years of formation. The monks shared meditation as a universal spiritual path – a way to peace, community, and solidarity with all people.

Following an introduction from the Abbot of Prinknash, Chris went on to study at the Dalai Lama's monastery in Dharamsala, India, deepening his understanding of meditation across contemplative traditions.

Since then, he has introduced Christian meditation to thousands of people across the UK and beyond.

The Missing Peace

For my children, Sophia and Theodore,
and my wife, Rachel.

The Missing Peace

*Meditation as a Spiritual Path to Peace,
Community and Oneness*

Chris Whittington

CANTERBURY
PRESS

© Chris Whittington 2025

Published in 2025 by Canterbury Press
Editorial office
3rd Floor, Invicta House,
110 Golden Lane,
London EC1Y 0TG, UK

https://canterburypress.hymnsam.co.uk/

Canterbury Press is an imprint of Hymns Ancient & Modern Ltd
(a registered charity)

Hymns Ancient & Modern® is a registered trademark of
Hymns Ancient & Modern Ltd
13A Hellesdon Park Road, Norwich,
Norfolk NR6 5DR, UK

All rights reserved. No part of this publication may be reproduced, stored in a retrieval system, or transmitted, in any form or by any means, electronic, mechanical, photocopying or otherwise, without the prior permission of the publisher, Canterbury Press.

Chris Whittington has asserted his right under the Copyright, Designs and Patents Act 1988 to be identified as the Author of this Work

British Library Cataloguing in Publication data
A catalogue record for this book is available from the British Library

ISBN 978-1-78622-679-2

EU GPSR Authorised Representative
LOGOS EUROPE, 9 rue Nicolas Poussin, 17000, LA ROCHELLE, France
E-mail: Contact@logoseurope.eu

No part of this book may be used or reproduced in any manner for the purpose of training artificial intelligence technologies or systems.

Typeset by Regent Typesetting

Biblical quotations marked NAB are from The New American Bible, revised edition © 2010, 1991, 1986, 1970 Confraternity of Christian Doctrine, Washington, D.C. and are used by permission of the copyright owner. All Rights Reserved. No part of the New American Bible may be reproduced in any form without permission in writing from the copyright owner.

Scripture quotations marked NRSVUK are from New Revised Standard Version Bible: Anglicized Edition, copyright © 1989, 1995 National Council of the Churches of Christ in the United States of America. Used by permission.
All rights reserved worldwide.
All other Bible quotations are the author's own translation.

Bible quotations marked DBH are from David Bentley Hart's translation of The New Testament © 2017, 2023 by David Bentley Hart. Reproduced with permission of The Licensor through PLSclear.

'Anthem' Words and Music by Leonard Cohen © 1992, Reproduced by permission of Sony/ATV Songs LLC/ Sony Music Publishing, London W1F 9LD.

CONTENTS

Acknowledgements   vii
Before you Begin   1

Part One: God is Our Being

  1 Accepting the Invitation to our Life   7
  2 Solitude, Compassion, Community   9
  3 The Peace we Seek is Already Here   11
  4 Prayer as Intimate Relationship   13
  5 'Come, and You Will See'   15

Part Two: Establishing Peace in Ourselves

  6 A Prayer Word Flowing with the Breath   21
  7 Stepping Back from the Flip Chart   26
  8 Greeting Thoughts with Stillness   27
  9 'Enter into your Inner Room'   30
10 In Returning and Rest, in Quietness and Trust   33
11 Trusting Simplicity, Trusting Silence   35
12 'I Began to Sense a Place of Peace and Freedom'   37
13 Walking Across the Waves   39
14 Meeting Difficult Emotions   41
15 'I'm Just an Anxious Person'   44
16 Taming our Inner Critic   47
17 Transforming our Fear   50
18 Stop Judging your Practice   53
19 'There's a Crack in Everything'   56
20 Flowers in the Desert   59
21 Walking by Faith, not by Sight   61

Part Three: Becoming Places of Peace

22	Being with God without any Agenda	67
23	The Opportunity of our Life	69
24	Enlightenment in Everyday Life	72
25	The Fruit of Self-forgetfulness	74
26	The Experience of Oneness	77
27	When Life becomes Prayer and Prayer becomes Life	79
28	In Your Light we See Light	82
29	*'Ephphatha!'* Be Opened!	84
30	A New Relationship with Time	87
31	Travelling Lightly – Living Fully	90
32	Seeing Creation as Radiance	93

Part Four: Peace in the World

33	Emptying Ourselves of Self	99
34	At-one-ment	102
35	Resting in Awareness	103
36	Silence and Solidarity	106
37	Touching Peace in Everyday Life	109
38	'Me-Time' Becomes 'Our-Time'	112
39	The Gift of Attention	115
40	The Gift of Peace	117
41	An Ecology of Love	119
42	Present-With, Present-For	122
43	'Blessed are the Peacemakers'	124

The School of Contemplative Life   128

ACKNOWLEDGEMENTS

I would like offer my heartfelt thanks to all who have helped bring this little book to publication; to the members of The School of Contemplative Life practice community, whose commitment to the practice, openness, testimony and compassion to each other has been and continues to be a source of inspiration and joy; to David Shervington, Rachel Geddes and Josie Gunn of Canterbury Press, and Kathleen McCully, for their enthusiastic encouragement and work on the manuscript; to those from our practice community who generously offered proofreading and editorial support, in particular Sara Lewis, and Tim and Kim Binder; and to Carla Cooper, Rachel Candlin, Revd Dr Janet Williams and Peter Ruxton, trustees of the School, for their continued support, encouragement and friendship.

Particular thanks go to Marksteen Adamson, Lizzie Botterill, Hannah Coles, Simon Dryland, Steven Tatlow and Kerry Mattholie of ASHA & Co. for the gift of their collective creativity, including the title and beautiful design of the book; to John Simmons for the delightful haiku interspersed throughout the book and whose early encouragement and advice were invaluable; and to my wife, Rachel, for her loving support and grounding presence.

Finally, I owe a deep debt of gratitude to the Benedictines of Prinknash Abbey Monastery, in particular Sylvester Houédard OSB, Stephen Horton OSB and Abbot Aldhelm Cameron-Brown OSB, and to Martin Laird OSA. There are no words to describe what they have taught me. Their gifts continue to unfold.

BEFORE YOU BEGIN

In a world that seems so fragmented and chaotic, the search for spiritual grounding, for the transcendent, for God, for inner and outer peace, has perhaps never been more important. We are faced with so many things that make peace (both within and without) seem almost impossible, or at least a little foolish to imagine. Many young people view the future with an increasing sense of foreboding. Others look with alarm at the crumbling of religious, civic and political institutions. Consumerism, materialism and distraction dominate so many aspects of our life. We see immense inequality and injustice, continuing conflict and violence. We are the first people in the history of our species to measure the finitude of natural resources and to witness their depletion and destruction from a global perspective. We gaze in wonder at increasingly spectacular images of the unfathomable immensity of the universe, while an increasing number of us experience uneasiness and dissatisfaction with religious formulations that appear intent on reducing all mystery to fixed propositions and statements of belief and pitching one way of faith against another.

In the words of Martin Laird OSA,

> While we continue to see fewer and fewer people regularly attending church services, their deep, genuine longing for the depth-dimension of Christianity has only grown through the years. Sadly, most Christians have absolutely no idea that Christianity has anything to say about this, much less that it has its own vibrant contemplative tradition. This is largely due to the fact that it has never been presented to them.

To all intents and purposes, the teaching and practice of meditation, of silent prayer, has all but disappeared from institutional churches.

What was once taught as a wisdom practice for engagement with, and the interpretation of, life and Scripture has been mostly forgotten. It's not surprising that so many seeking spiritual wisdom today are unsure where to find it. This was my experience until I discovered (or was led to) Prinknash Abbey Benedictine Monastery in Gloucestershire, England. In so many ways, I felt I had come home. A year before I went to live with the Benedictine community at Prinknash when I was 19, I had a conversation with Abbot Aldhelm which profoundly influenced the direction of my life (though it took me many years to realize how deeply). The Abbot said very little, but was an excellent teacher. He taught as much by his gentle presence and the silences between his words. Before discovering Prinknash, I had no one to speak with about what I was encountering, which was at the same time both utterly irresistible and profoundly disorienting. I hadn't been brought up in a religious family, and my attempts to speak about this with my friends left them completely nonplussed. Alongside texts from the Christian contemplative tradition, I'd been studying texts from other traditions, particularly those of Zen and Tibetan Buddhism, Advaita Vedanta and Sufi Islam. I told the Abbot it seemed as if a single voice was shining through everything I was reading. I can still remember the wave of excitement and relief I felt when he just smiled and quietly said, 'Yes.' Another time as we were walking in the abbey grounds, I told the Abbot I imagined people of different faiths and none, speaking different languages, wearing different clothes, coming together to practise meditation, and how, in the depths of their shared silence, they might touch the silent ground of peace in God beyond all distinctions. That afterwards, returning to where words have beginnings and endings again, they would still be speaking their different languages, wearing their different clothes, but something would have changed. That to someone looking on, not a great deal may seem to have happened. But they might notice how comfortable people are with each other, content to speak or simply enjoy a cup of tea and each other's company in silence. That they would almost certainly notice the deep atmosphere of peace. Abbot Aldhelm looked into my eyes and said, 'I think so too.' I felt another great wave of excitement and relief.

Our hope is that this little book will help people discover an ancient jewel within the riches of a contemplative tradition which might be described as the missing piece of much contemporary Christianity – to offer a simple guide for those who wish to explore the open waters of meditation and discover the silent wellspring of peace and compassion to be found within each of us. The book is largely formed from short talks given to The School of Contemplative Life weekly online practice community (details of which can be found at the end of the book).

The use of short, self-contained chapters (often one or two pages in length) is intended both to provide an accessible resource to the reader and to support them in establishing and maintaining a daily meditation practice. It is not meant to be read from beginning to end in one sitting. We invite you to approach it slowly, gently, perhaps returning to the same words several times. You might pause between sentences. Allowing moments of silence can help us engage with a deeper quality of attention. Rather than trying to analyse, we can allow things to unfold, to 'speak' in their own time, perhaps not in words but in the silence, through the silence. Part One provides some essential framing and foundational points of orientation, such as that God is not something separate from us, but more intimately present than we can imagine. We look at how meditation was practised by the Desert Fathers and Mothers, following the teaching and example of Jesus. In Part Two we explore the essential skills and disciplines of meditation which help bring the mind to stillness and unveil the silent ground of our being in God. We look at how our noisy, distracted minds create the illusion that we are separate from God, from each other and the world, and how meditation can help us overcome this illusion. We look at how to acknowledge and meet all that life offers and throws at us with less struggle and resistance, to cultivate a new relationship with life and those around us, characterized by greater awareness, freedom and compassion. In Parts Three and Four the focus broadens from the necessary initial work of establishing peace in ourselves to becoming *places of peace* in the world. We explore how meditation contributes to and flowers within the ethical life (rather than simply being about individual 'wellness' or 'self-improvement'), that the focus of meditation is not to obtain an extraordinary life for ourselves, but to live our ordinary life extraordinarily well, *together*, and that the source and end of meditation (like all prayer) is *relationship*, love.

There has perhaps never been a more urgent need to discover afresh the contemplative heart within each of us, to establish peace in ourselves that we may be places of peace in the world. Are the wisdom practices of the contemplative tradition merely optional extras for the Christian? Quite the opposite, says Rowan Williams:

> Contemplation is very far from being just one kind of thing that Christians do: it is the key to prayer, liturgy, art and ethics, the key to the essence of a renewed humanity that is capable of seeing the world and other subjects in the world with freedom – freedom from self-oriented, acquisitive habits and the distorted understanding that comes from them.[1]

Meditation in the Christian wisdom tradition is a quiet path to being fully awake and gratefully present. As we learn to be still, to be silent, as we learn to let go of our search for what was never missing, we come home to the boundless love which has held us in its embrace from all eternity.

---

[1] Rowan Williams, 'Archbishop Rowan Williams Address to the Synod of Bishops', *Zenit*, 11 October 2012, https://zenit.org/2012/10/11/archbishop-rowan-williams-address-to-the-synod-of-bishops/, accessed 19.03.2025.

PART ONE

GOD IS OUR BEING

*There's a peace within
you need never be without.
God waits there for you.*

1

ACCEPTING THE INVITATION TO OUR LIFE

God is our being.[1] This astonishing message about the deepest truth of who we are is a crucial point of orientation for how we understand meditation in the Christian tradition, its prayer of stillness and of silence. Just as a ray of light cannot be separate from its source, we cannot be separate from God, who is the very life of our life. 'The most beautiful and the greatest learning', says Clement of Alexandria, 'is to know oneself. For whoever knows their self knows God. And whoever knows God becomes like Him.'[2] We don't need to invite God into our life. Rather, we need to accept *God's* invitation to our life in him. Ultimately, all we are doing in meditation is accepting the invitation to 'the most beautiful and the greatest learning' about who we are. We are not trying to *obtain* anything (what is there to obtain when God is our being?). We are turning to that which is more intimately present to us than we are to ourselves.

As one of the most popular spiritual writers of the twentieth century, Cistercian monk Thomas Merton, reminds us,

> In prayer we discover what we already have. You start from where you are, and you deepen what you already have, and

---

[1] *The Book of Privy Counselling*, Chapter 1, in *The Cloud of Unknowing and Other Works*, trans. A. C. Spearing (London: Penguin Books, 2001), p. 104.

[2] Clement of Alexandria, *Paedagogus*, Book 3, quoted in *The Kiss: The Beshara Talks of Dom Sylvester Houédard* (Cheltenham: Beshara Publications, 2022), p. 205 (translation altered slightly).

you realize you are already there. We already have everything, but we don't know it and don't experience it. Everything has been given to us. All we need to do is experience what we already possess.³

After realizing that all he was searching for had always been within him, St Augustine wrote:

> You were within me, but I was outside. There I sought you, as I rushed about among the beautiful things you had made. You were with me, but I was not with you. The beautiful things of this world kept me far from you. You called. You cried. You burst through my deafness. You scattered my blindness.⁴

If we can't see this now, we need not worry. As St Paul reassures us, we will come to see 'face to face' and 'know fully, as [we] have been fully known' (1 Cor. 13.12, NRSVUK). What will we see? What will we know? That God is our being, that we are light from light.⁵ In meditation, we accept God's invitation to discover who we are, to become who we are.

---

³ Quoted by Martin Laird, *Into the Silent Land: The Practice of Contemplation* (London: Darton, Longman and Todd, 2006), p. 53.

⁴ Translation by Benignus O'Rourke, *Finding Your Hidden Treasure* (London: Darton, Longman and Todd, 2010), p. 22.

⁵ In the words of the Nicene Creed.

2

SOLITUDE, COMPASSION, COMMUNITY

Solitary prayer is the most emphasized aspect of Jesus' prayer life in the New Testament. Matthew, Mark and Luke all provide examples in their Gospels of Jesus frequently withdrawing to a solitary or deserted place to pray. Jesus teaches the central importance of silent, intimate communion with God in solitude. 'To be contemplative as Christ is contemplative', said Rowan Williams, 'is to be open to all the fullness that the Father wishes to pour into our hearts. With our minds made still and ready to receive, with our self-generated fantasies about God and ourselves reduced to silence, we are at last at the point where we may begin to grow.'[1] The practice of meditation in the Christian tradition has its foundation in the teachings and prayer life of Jesus.[2] The Gospel writers skilfully record a pattern of solitary prayer, engaged compassion and the creation of community, presenting these aspects of Jesus' life alongside each other like beams of light radiating from a single source, harmonious, inseparable.

Early in Luke's Gospel, we hear how Jesus would withdraw to deserted places to pray (Luke 5.16). Luke very carefully places Jesus' withdrawal to solitude between two stories of healing, and these stories of healing are themselves placed between stories of Jesus forming a community as he invites people to follow him. A little

---

[1] Rowan Williams, 'Archbishop Rowan Williams Address to the Synod of Bishops', *Zenit*, 11 October 2012, https://zenit.org/2012/10/11/archbishop-rowan-williams-address-to-the-synod-of-bishops/, accessed 19.03.2025.

[2] I am very grateful to Martin Laird OSA, whose generously shared reflections informed and helped form this chapter.

later in Luke's Gospel, we are told how Jesus spends a night in prayer alone on a mountain before he chooses the Twelve Apostles (Luke 6.12–13).

In the Gospel of Matthew, Jesus withdraws in a boat to a deserted place after he hears of the death of John the Baptist. The crowds soon find out where he has gone and they follow him. And when Jesus sees the vast crowd, he is moved deeply with compassion and heals the sick (Matt. 14.13–15). As evening falls, the disciples ask Jesus to send the crowds away so they can buy food for themselves in nearby villages. But Jesus replies, 'They have no need to go away; you give them something to eat' (Matt. 14.16, DBH). Then follows the miracle of the multiplication of loaves and fishes – the miracle of a compassionate sharing of resources, so no one goes hungry. After everyone has been fed, Jesus tells his disciples to take a boat and go before him to the other side of the lake while he dismisses the crowds. As soon as he has dismissed them, he ascends the mountain by himself to pray. When evening comes, he is there alone.

We see the same pattern at the beginning of Mark's Gospel. Waking early before dawn, Jesus leaves his companions and goes to a deserted place to pray. Knowing what Jesus would be doing, Simon and the others go to find him and tell Jesus that everyone is looking for him. Jesus immediately suggests they should go to the nearby villages, where he can teach and heal, because this is his purpose for coming (Mark 1.35–39).

The Gospel writers quite clearly connect Jesus' distinctive way of solitary prayer with his ministry of teaching, healing and the creation of community. There is no need for Jesus' most emphasized and distinctive way of prayer to remain one of Western Christianity's best-kept secrets. Together we can make it known. We can share this precious gift with the world.

3

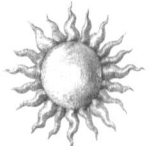

THE PEACE WE SEEK IS ALREADY HERE

Our culture is overwhelmingly about acquiring things. We are bombarded with a constant stream of messages telling us that in order to be successful, in order to have value, to matter, we need to get hold of things: qualifications, the right career, the right body shape, partner, house and (of course) money. So too with peace. If we want peace, we need to add this to the list of things we lack and need to acquire. It couldn't be more different with meditation in the Christian tradition. At the heart of the Christian message is a simple, radical, often challenging and sometimes mind-boggling message: we don't need to acquire anything. The peace we seek is already here, buried in the field of our life like a precious jewel, even if, for a great deal of the time, our lives can feel very far from peaceful. So, why is this peace hidden from us so much of the time? The short answer is, because we cover it with a veil of mental noise and clutter. We lose sight of it, then look for it in the wrong place, in the wrong way, using the wrong tools. We search outside ourselves when the jewel of peace is all the time in the pocket of our heart.

The great seventh-century teacher of prayer St Isaac the Syrian understood the kingdom of heaven to mean the gift of contemplation, the gift of seeing clearly, of transfigured awareness. With this in mind, we might look again at when Jesus was asked when the kingdom of God would come, as if it wasn't here and might suddenly appear at the right time in the future. He answered, 'The coming of the Kingdom cannot be observed, and no one will announce, "Look, here it is," or, "There it is." For behold, the Kingdom of God is within you' (Luke 17.20–21, NAB).

It's easy to pass over how deeply challenging Jesus' answer was. It's equally easy to overlook the life-changing invitation wrapped within his words. The kingdom is not going to 'come', because it's already present, within us. The kingdom cannot be observed by the thinking, conceptualizing mind. Just as the eye which sees cannot see itself, the kingdom cannot be made into an object of awareness, because it is that which sees, awareness itself – pristine, luminous, the imageless image of God. The kingdom of awareness cannot be observed by the discursive, conceptualizing mind, but it can be known by the heart, by means of a simple, loving intention. At this threshold the mind must fall silent, and allow love to carry us over.

4

PRAYER AS INTIMATE RELATIONSHIP

A few years ago, I was asked to speak about meditation at a weekend camp for young Christians on a farm near my hometown of Cheltenham, England. Most of the weekend's activities were held in a large barn converted into a beautiful event space, a stone's throw from the massed tents. I wasn't surprised when I was allocated a slot late on the Saturday afternoon in a small medieval church a few hundred metres from the main site. I knew that the ancient way of silent prayer I'd be speaking about would be unknown to almost everyone there. I would have been pleased with ten people coming along. A few minutes before the session was due to start, 200 people appeared, squeezed onto the ancient pews, filled the dark oak choir stalls and sat cross-legged on the floor, filling every available space. The little church was packed. I struck a small prayer bell and the clear, bright sound called everyone to silence.

After resting in the silence together for a few minutes, I asked if anyone knew anything about intimate relationships. More than a few people smiled. And the silence in the tiny crowded church deepened.

Then I asked if anyone had experienced the wonderful, heady excitement of meeting someone you think is absolutely gorgeous. You want to know them. You want them to know you. You can't get them out of your head. You want to see them as much as possible and to talk and talk and talk. 'What's your favourite film?' 'What's the best place you've travelled to?' 'What's your favourite book, food, anything?' The silence deepened further.

Then I asked if anyone had experienced a relationship that had gone beyond this delightful early phase, and come to the point where the depth and synergy and intimacy were now perhaps best known and expressed in moments of silence – those blessed moments when words fall away and you just look at your beloved and adore them, and receive their adoring gaze.

Then I asked: why, if we know this is true of our relationships with each other, would we ever imagine that prayer, that our relationship with God, would be any different?

5

'COME, AND YOU WILL SEE'

Meditation trains the mind. It is an ancient way of responding to Christ's invitation, 'Come, and you will see' (John 1.39, NAB). What will we see? We will see that we are not separate from God, or from each other, or from the whole of creation, but one in God's oneness: 'I have given them the glory that you gave me, so that they may be one just as we are one; I am in them and you in me, that they may be brought to completion as one' (John 17.22–23).

For Christians, meditation is also an ancient way of prayer, described by one of the most insightful teachers of the early Church, the great Desert Father Evagrius, as 'the laying aside of concepts',[1] the letting go of thoughts.[2] The focus of meditation is not to obtain an extraordinary life (however we might imagine that for ourselves or for others), but to live our ordinary life extraordinarily well. It's about seeing clearly and acting with compassion. It's about wholeness and relationship. The simple practice is not the preserve of specialists and it cannot be owned by one group or another. Whether we are five years old or 95, have a PhD or cannot read, the wisdom and healing processes of meditation are available to all of us. It's profoundly egalitarian.

Much of contemporary culture and education is directed towards cultivating the gifts of the thinking, conceptualizing mind.

---

[1] Evagrius Ponticus, *The Praktikos and Chapters on Prayer*, Cistercian Studies Series 4 (Kalamazoo, MI: Cistercian Publications, 1981), Chapter 57.

[2] By 'thoughts' in this book I also mean feelings, sensations and perceptions (such as sights, sounds, textures, tastes and smells), all that you might speak of as the content of experience.

Overwhelming priority and status are given to this important but surface aspect of ourselves. While necessary to negotiate and enjoy daily life (it helped you find this book), an over-preoccupation with the content of this surface life has some serious risks attached to it. Almost without realizing it, our attention can become fixated on the waves of thoughts that arise in reaction to the content of our moment-to-moment experience. Captivated and held captive by these waves, we become like small boats trying to navigate the swell, tossed about and occasionally overwhelmed. All too easily we come to believe that these waves are who we are. We lose all sense of the ocean, of the depthless depths of our life, 'hidden with Christ in God' (Col. 3.3, NRSVUK). Many people experience this as a sense of separation and dislocation, as if they are living at a distance from their life, from those around them and from God. But just as thoughts cannot be separate from the awareness in which they appear, we cannot be separate from God, the One in whom 'we live and move and have our being' (Acts 17.28, NRSVUK).

Most of us, for a large part of our lives, react to life's events on a sort of autopilot, running along well-worn tracks of reactive habit, automatically spinning commentary (chatting to ourselves) in reaction to the appearance of simple thoughts and feelings. We are mostly unaware that we are doing this or that our relationship with life could be radically different. This old monastic tale speaks very clearly about this and its (not infrequent) consequences:

> Two monks were walking between monasteries. They came to a ford in a river they needed to cross and saw that it had become swollen by heavy rain. Standing by the ford was a young woman, crying. Between her sobs, she told the monks that if she couldn't get across the river to sell some goods at a nearby market, her family would have nothing to eat. Without hesitation the older monk picked her up, put her on his back, and waded across the river, using his staff to help him. Once across he put the young woman down and, in her delight, she gave him a large hug. Now, the younger monk was not happy at all with what had happened. And as the two monks continued their journey, the young monk chewed

and chewed on his anger until he felt he might burst. A short distance on, unable to contain himself any longer, he leapt in front of the older monk and shouted, 'Have you forgotten your vows? How could you touch that young woman? What sort of monk are you?'

The old monk calmly replied, 'I saw someone in trouble. I carried her across the river and I put her down. You are still carrying her.'

As we learn to greet our thoughts and feelings and the content of our experience with greater stillness, with greater silence, the apparent confines of our world begin to dissolve. A space of opportunity opens in which to better see those around us, their needs and their mysterious beauty and dignity. In the following chapters we will explore two essential disciplines of meditation which help to bring the reactive mind to stillness and unveil the silent ground of our being in God: inner concentration (un-grasping, focused attention) and opening awareness.

Meditation is a school of community, a school of oneness, a quiet path to being fully awake and gratefully present. The simple practice helps us turn to what is before all our words and ideas, before all religious metaphors and doctrines, and opens us to the peace which transfigures all that divides us and lays bare who we are – members of one family, living in one shared home.

'Come, and you will see.'

Part Two

ESTABLISHING PEACE IN OURSELVES

*Why go search for God
as if he would hide? He's here
inside you, waiting.*

6

A PRAYER WORD FLOWING WITH THE BREATH

Most of us will have experienced the dramatic effect that unrestrained thoughts and mental noise can have on our life. This was very well known to the early Christian contemplatives of the Egyptian and Syrian deserts. The Desert Fathers and Mothers, as they came to be known, saw in Jesus' own temptation in the desert (Matt. 4.1–11) a simple but radically effective way of responding to the pull of our thoughts and cultivating stillness and peace in the face of them. Each time Jesus was tempted with a different form of power, he refused to enter into an internal dialogue with the tempting thought. Instead, he simply recited Scripture, and kept reciting Scripture for as long as was necessary to escape the inner chatter that so easily holds us captive, as we react to a thought with more and more thoughts. Following the example of Jesus, these early Christian contemplatives developed the practice of reciting a prayer word or phrase to help bring the discursive (chattering) mind to greater and greater stillness and enter into silent prayer. 'Contain your mind within the words of prayer', says the seventh-century abbot St John Climacus. Climacus is also one of many teachers who suggest that the saying of the prayer word be combined with the flow of the breath.

Many people, if they were asked to say something about prayer, might describe something quite different from ordinary daily life. They might be surprised to hear Thomas Merton say, 'My God, I pray to you better by breathing. I pray to you better by walking than by talking.'[1] Something as ordinary as our breathing can become our prayer. Merton begins his advice to those seeking God with the words of St Paul, 'Pray without ceasing.' What might this mean? How might we go about this? 'It is really quite simple', says Merton. 'It is just as if Our Lord told us, "You must keep on breathing…"'[2] This ancient wisdom is a rich teaching for us today as we struggle to live well in our world of noise and distraction. The steady flow of our breath can become the steady flow of our prayer, the steady flow of a life which is *becoming* prayer. This most common form of Christian meditation – the gentle concentration and focusing of the mind to facilitate the opening of awareness, the saying of a prayer word in union with the breath – is the practice we will explore in this book.

When I was first introduced to meditation by Father Alphege of Prinknash Abbey, I threw my 19-year-old self into daily practice with a great deal of excited, self-conscious energy. The abbey was wonderfully quiet, with very few external distractions. No doubt this was very helpful in bringing me rapidly face to face with my inner noise and distractedness. A week later I told Father Alphege that I'd experienced a slightly uncomfortable feeling in my chest a few times. He gave me one of his famous smiles and said, 'Relax. You're trying too hard. Let the prayer word and your breath flow together gently, and rest there.' The discomfort went away and never returned.

If we're trying to paint a window frame without painting the window at the same time, or to remove an irritating speck of dust from our eye, our breathing naturally slows and deepens without any conscious instruction. The steady flow of our breath contributes greatly to our focus and concentration. Whether we are trying to undertake a delicate task or experiencing a sudden eruption of anxiety, we easily recognize the wisdom and healing anchor of the breath. So, too, the skilful use of the breath helps greatly with the deepening of our meditation practice, whether it is combined with the use of a prayer word or used simply on its own. The breath becomes a bridge which unites our whole being. It is the energy

---

[1] Thomas Merton, *Entering the Silence: Becoming a Monk & Writer* (Harper Collins ebooks, 1996), p. 161.

[2] Thomas Merton, *A Balanced Life of Prayer*, p. 4, published on the Merton Center website: https://merton.org/ITMS/Annual/08/Merton1-21.pdf

of concentration, of un-grasping, focused attention which facilitates the opening of awareness. Over time, our breathing during meditation naturally deepens and slows (three to five breaths a minute is common) and the centre of our breathing moves down from the chest to the abdomen. Just to follow our breath helps guide us to the silent depths of our being, where we might say to God with St Augustine, 'I breathed your fragrance.'[3]

The wisdom of the breath has great power. Over time, the prayer word and breath become one harmonious flow. As this happens, there are likely to be moments when our self-conscious mind falls away. Meditation continues, but there is no meditator present. Prayer continues, but we are *being* prayed. As St John of the Cross says so beautifully, 'The soul that is united and transformed in God breathes God with the same divine breathing with which God, while in her, breathes her in himself.'[4] All that is left is *one* breath, *one* breathing, *one* flow of love. The Risen Christ says to the disciples, '"Peace be with you. As the Father has sent me, so I send you." And when he had said this, he breathed on them and said to them, "Receive the Holy Spirit"' (John 20.21–2, NRSVUK). Christ gives the Holy Spirit by breathing and says, in effect, 'Breathe what I have given you. Breathe the gift I am always breathing within you.'

Meditation, like gardening, is really about collaboration. We often talk about growing this or that ('I love to grow radishes', 'I grew a wonderful crop of potatoes last summer') and it's fine to talk like this. But it's useful to remind ourselves from time to time that we don't actually grow anything at all, that things are quite happy to grow themselves. Our practice is never more than opening to what God is doing, helping to create the best conditions for growth to happen.

The basics of meditation in the Christian tradition are very simple.

---

[3] St Augustine, *Confessions*, Book 10 XXVII, translation in Benignus O'Rourke, *Finding Your Hidden Treasure* (London: Darton, Longman and Todd, 2010), p. 22.

[4] St John of the Cross, The Spiritual Canticle, Red A., str. 38, quoted by Martin Laird in *Into the Silent Land: The Practice of Contemplation* (London: Darton, Longman and Todd, 2006), p. 18.

Sit in a solid, erect posture, with your back as straight as you are able, your body still, relaxed, but alert.

Once you are sitting comfortably, begin by closing your eyes gently and taking a few slightly slower, slightly deeper breaths, bringing your attention to the flow of your breath. Breathe in from the abdomen and breathe out fully. Some initial deeper breaths can help gather our attention, settle the mind and bring us to stillness. Both the inbreath and the outbreath should be steady and unforced, so that if you had a little glass mirror under your nose it would hardly cloud at all. Then, let your breathing return to its natural flow. Sometimes when people first start to use the breath, they become very conscious of how they are breathing. Sometimes they wonder if the breath is deep enough, at other times whether it is slow enough, or not quite right in some way. If you find yourself with thoughts like this, just let them go and trust your body. It has all the wisdom it needs. It knows what to do. Let it show you. It takes just a few days for your body to teach you all you need to know.

Next, begin to repeat a prayer word or short prayer phrase silently, interiorly, in unison with the flow of your breath. If your prayer word is one syllable (such as 'Love' or 'God' or 'Peace'), say the word with the inbreath and with the outbreath. If your prayer word or phrase has more than one syllable, say the first syllable (or group of words) with the inbreath, and the second syllable (or group of words) with the outbreath. During our time of meditation (a good guideline is to practise twice a day for at least 20 to 25 minutes), we give our whole attention to the repetition of the prayer word, allowing the repetition and the flow of the breath to become a single flow. The crucial thing is to find what is most comfortable for you (what is most likely to help you forget yourself) and stay with that. Nothing should be forced or laboured.

Whenever you notice that your attention has followed a thought or feeling (or some other content of experience), just gently bring your attention back to saying your word in the flow of your breath. You will be distracted from your practice. It's going to happen. Don't fight it! We are not trying *not* to have thoughts (a common and very unhelpful myth about meditation). We are learning to have a new, more spacious relationship with our thoughts and the content of our experience, characterized by greater peace, by greater freedom and compassion.

The practice is simply to return our attention to the practice each time we notice we have become distracted. We just notice and return, without comment, without judgement. To notice we are distracted is not *failure*. It is *awareness*. To notice we have been distracted 100 times is to have had 100 moments of awareness, 100 opportunities to come home.

All we need to do is to begin and to keep beginning, to return and to keep returning, releasing ourselves into our practice, into God's care, trusting we lack nothing.

7

STEPPING BACK FROM THE FLIP CHART

Some years ago, I was asked by a diocese to speak about meditation at their annual school leaders conference. Meditation in the Christian tradition (or any tradition) was completely new to most people present. As it turned out, the conference took place just a week before the first national Covid-19 lockdown, and everyone was deeply concerned about the possible impact of the virus, so I tried to make our time together as straightforward and practical as possible. I began by writing PROBLEM in large black letters on a flipchart and asked for a volunteer to stand just a few inches in front of it. When I asked what she could see, she replied, 'PROBLEM.' Then I asked if she could take a step back and tell us what she could see. This time she replied, 'PROBLEM, and a little bit of the room.' Each time she stepped back she could see more of the room. She could still see PROBLEM, of course. It was there in big black letters. It wasn't going away. Life has a habit of happening and it needs to be faced. But with each step back, her field of vision opened and her relationship to PROBLEM changed. With each step, she was encountering the PROBLEM in an expanded, more spacious context.

During our periods of meditation practice we learn to step back, to come into a new relationship with whatever happens to be flowing through our mind. We don't try to suppress our thoughts, our feelings, the content of our experience, or to run away or hide from them. We simply greet what arises without comment and return to our practice. In this simple way, in learning to step back, we enter a more spacious and peaceful relationship with life. We discover a space of opportunity in which we have more freedom to decide *how* we want to relate to all that life offers us, or throws at us.

8

GREETING THOUGHTS WITH STILLNESS

There are times when it can feel almost impossible to find some peace from the noise of our thoughts. I can remember a particularly challenging time when I was living at Prinknash Abbey. I told the Novice Master that I felt completely unable to control the waves of thoughts that were tormenting me. He offered some simple advice and suggested I read a book which had recently made a deep impression on him. The advice came as a complete surprise. 'Stop trying to control your thoughts.' The book was a collection of wonderfully simple, practical talks by the Zen teacher Shunryu Suzuki, and the Novice Master closed our conversation by reading a few lines from it.

> To give your sheep or cow a large spacious meadow is the best way to control him … let them do what they want, and watch them. This is the best policy. To ignore them is not good; that is the worst policy. The second worst is trying to control them. The best way is to watch them, just to watch them, without trying to control them.[1]

Thoughts will arise quite naturally, as naturally as clouds in the sky. There is very little we can do about that. The challenges we face flow from how we *react* to our thoughts. And we can do a considerable amount about this. In his work *On Watchfulness and Holiness*,[2] St

---

[1] Shunryu Suzuki, *Zen Mind, Beginner's Mind* (Boulder, CO: Shambala Publications, 1970), p. 15.

[2] *On Watchfulness and Holiness* in *The Philokalia*, Vol. 1 (London: Faber and Faber, 1983).

Hesychios writes with great insight about how we routinely engage with our thoughts at lightning speed, on a sort of unconscious autopilot. Hesychios teaches a simple way to meet our thoughts wisely, noting four steps in a reactive process that can take us quickly from our initial encounter with a thought, through to a concrete act we might have wished to avoid. I suspect that most of us will have no problem recognizing these steps in our own experience.

Step 1   A simple thought pops up in our head. Everything that follows is the story of our reactive engagement with this initial thought.

Step 2   We rush at lightning speed to look at the initial thought. We embrace it with the arms of our attention and immediately begin chatting to ourselves about it, busily wrapping it with more and more thoughts.

Step 3   The third step is our agreement with the story (the film) we have whipped up in our heads in reaction to the simple initial thought.

Step 4   The final step is the concrete action to which the whole process has led us, and which flows from the story we created.

In describing these steps, Hesychios is hoping we might learn to recognize and pause this reactive process at an early point, preventing the proverbial snowball running down the hill, picking up more and more snow until it is too large for us to manage.

In meditation, we don't ignore thoughts or try to control them. This just gives them energy and further binds our attention to them. We are learning to quietly acknowledge thoughts and skilfully manage our reaction to them. And we do this through the simple means of greeting thoughts peacefully, with stillness and with silence. Each time we notice our attention has raced off to embrace a thought and we are busily chatting to ourselves about it, we simply return our attention to our practice. We gently refuse to engage with the thought any further, and we let it go on its way. As Suzuki once said,

'Leave your front door and your back door open. Let thoughts come and go. Just don't serve them tea.'[3]

Establishing a more peaceful relationship with our thoughts is the foundation of a more peaceful relationship with our life. God will help us in this, says Hesychios, for:

> as the person who looks at the sun has their eyes filled with light, so the person who always gazes intently into their heart cannot fail to be illumined ... The mind that is constantly watched over, protected from engagement with the forms, images and fantasies that arise within it, is conditioned by nature to give birth from within itself to thoughts filled with light.[4]

---

[3] Shunryu Suzuki, David Chadwick (ed.), *Zen Is Right Now – More Teaching Stories and Anecdotes of Shunryu Suzuki* (Boulder, CO: Shambhala Publications, 2021), p. 45.

[4] Suzuki, *Zen is Right Now*, p. 45.

9

'ENTER INTO YOUR INNER ROOM'

Immediately before teaching us the Lord's Prayer (Matt. 6.9–13), Jesus introduces us to a way of prayer which resonates deeply with his practice of communing with God in solitude and silence. When we pray like this, we should not do so in a way that can be seen, that draws attention to what we are doing – including our own attention, as we get caught up in trying to watch our own progress: 'But when you pray, enter into your inner room and, having closed the door, pray to your Father in secret. And your Father who sees in secret will reward you' (Matt. 6.6). In meditation, we focus our whole attention on silently reciting our prayer word in unison with the flow of our breath. By this simple means we lift our attention off ourselves. We leave the *outer* rooms of self-conscious preoccupation, and enter the *inner* room of self-forgetful awareness, to pray in silent ('secret') communion with God. As prayer deepens, it becomes less and less a matter of what *we* think about, what *we* do, and increasingly a matter of simply being, of resting within what *God* is doing.

The anonymous medieval author of the *Book of Privy Counselling* outlines this wonderfully simple practice of entering the inner room of our being and resting there in silent, grateful awareness:

> When we turn to this work of contemplation, we should not think about what we are going to do next. When thoughts arise (as they will), we should lay them aside, regardless of whether they appear to be good thoughts or not-so-good thoughts. Release all that arises in the surface mind and rest

in a naked intent reaching out to God, without clothing this intent with any thought about God.

Let God be God and be content to accept that he is as he is without forcing God into any other shape or seeking to understand him with intellectual cleverness. Trust that God is God and let this be your foundation.

Accept this naked intent, rooted in trust, to be nothing but a blind awareness of your own existence, as if you were inwardly saying to God, 'That I exist, Lord, I offer to you, with no thought about you.' It's as if you're saying to God: 'That I am, Lord, I offer to you, without adding any thought about you, but simply accepting you as you are – and nothing beyond that.'

Add no thoughts about yourself, just as you do not add any thoughts about God, so that you may be one with him in awareness, without any division or scattering of mind. For God is your being, and you are what you are in him.

And so, in this work of contemplation, open your mind to God as you do to yourself, and to yourself as you do to God, accepting that he is as he is and you are as you are, so that your thoughts are not dispersed or divided, but one in him who is All.

He is the ground of being both to himself and to all things; and that all things have their being in him and he is the being of all things means that he is one in all things and all things are in his oneness.

In this way shall your thoughts and feelings be oned[1] with him in grace without separation, if all your curious thinking about the attributes of your mysterious being, and of his, are pushed far back; so that your thought may be naked and your awareness unclouded, and you, in your nakedness, by the touching of grace, may be secretly sustained in your awareness by him simply as he is and beyond your seeing ...

---

[1] Oned ('oynd'), a Middle English term indicating the realization of our essential oneness with God.

Look up then lightly, and say to your Lord, whether in words or in the silent purpose of your heart: 'That I am, Lord, I offer to you, for it is you.' And be aware, nakedly, plainly and simply that you are as you are, without anything added.[2]

In meditation, we dwell in God in the simple gift of our being. We offer ourselves and receive ourselves in the silent prayer of naked awareness.

---

[2] My translation from the Middle English edition of *The Cloud of Unknowing and The Book of Privy Counselling*, edited by Phyllis Hodgson (Oxford: Oxford University Press for the Early English Text Society, 1981), pp. 135–7 (text altered slightly).

10

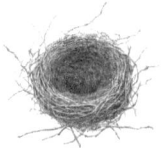

IN RETURNING AND REST, IN QUIETNESS AND TRUST

In the book of Isaiah we are given a wonderful summary of the simple heart of prayer: 'In returning and rest you shall be saved, in quietness and trust your strength lies' (Isa. 30.15). In returning and in rest, in quietness and in trust, God leads us to the silent depths of who we are in him, the depths of his love for us.

The essence of prayer is radically simple, yet most of us will have encountered how, for various reasons, it can be difficult to accept this and release ourselves into its welcoming simplicity. For a whole host of reasons, we can try and complicate prayer. Often it is the radical simplicity of the silent prayer of meditation that people can initially find challenging. As one of my first teachers would often say, it is meditation, not the simple and obvious truth to which meditation is a gate, that people find difficult.

When we begin to meditate, it can be quite a surprise to see our distractedness and restlessness reflected in the mirror of our practice. But each time we see this, we have a precious opportunity to come back to our prayer word, to our breath, and to rest there. We can turn to the ever-present peace within which our thoughts and feelings appear. Some books can give the impression that prayer is quite a complicated business. We might have been told at some time that we need to do this or that, or understand this or that, in order to pray well. In various ways, prayer can be presented as if there is a lot of ground to cover to be in the right place with God. But there is no ground to cover. As a wave cannot be separate from the ocean, we cannot be separate from God. God is the ground of our being, the life of our life. If this were not so, we would not exist.

We don't need to find any special way of getting in touch with God. Rather, we need to let go of any notions of prayer that cause us to think otherwise. There's no special mystical key we need to get hold of in order to unlock any special mystical door. As we read in the book of Revelation, 'Behold, there is an open door before you, which no one can close' (Rev. 3.8).

We have a tendency to want to complicate what is simple, while all God wants to do through the simplicity of meditation is to simplify *us*, to help us return from distractedness to wholeness, to know the love which is our very being. In the words of St John of the Cross, it is enough to 'preserve a loving awareness of God, with no desire to feel or understand any particular thing about God.'[1]

---

[1] *The Collected Works of St John of the Cross*, trans. Kieran Kavanaugh and Otilio Rodriguez (Washington DC: Institute of Carmelite Studies, 1991), p. 92.

11

TRUSTING SIMPLICITY, TRUSTING SILENCE

As the Carmelite Ruth Burrows writes in her precious book *The Essence of Prayer*, 'Basing ourselves on what Jesus shows us of God (and we Christians have only one teacher, Jesus the Christ who is our Way), we must realize that what we have to do is allow ourselves to be loved, to be there for Love to love us.'[1] These are tremendously encouraging words. But how do we deal practically with our tendency to want to complicate prayer? How can we simply be here, present in the present, and allow ourselves to be loved? Well, this is where trust comes in. It requires great trust to return our attention to where our bodies are, to where our life actually is, and remain here in stillness and quietness. It takes trust to set out on a way of prayer that is about handing the controls back to God (though they were, of course, never anywhere else). It takes trust to lift our attention *off* ourselves.

Prayer is not primarily something *we* do, but what *God* is doing, within us and for us, at a depth that we cannot see. Prayer, says St John of the Cross, happens 'secretly in darkness, hidden from the faculties ... so hidden that the mind cannot speak of it.'[2] It largely doesn't register in the self-conscious mind. This is why we cannot and should not try to judge our practice and should avoid getting caught up in worries about whether we are praying correctly. No wonder the ego can sometimes object to meditation with great

---

[1] Ruth Burrows, *The Essence of Prayer* (London: Burns & Oates, 2006), p. 3.
[2] St John of the Cross, quoted by Burrows, *The Essence of Prayer*, p. 8.

energy, creativity and persistence.³ This aspect of ourselves wants things to register loudly and clearly. It wants to be entertained. It wants *prayer* to be entertaining. Ego will try to keep one hand (or even better, two) on what it imagines are the controls of prayer. It cannot succeed, of course. As prayer is primarily what God is doing and we participate in, it cannot be grasped or controlled in any way. But we can find ourselves being urged by the ego to go searching around for more entertaining forms of prayer, looking outside ourselves for what is ceaselessly happening within. All we need to do is sit quietly, trusting that we are in the right place, trusting that we are perfectly acceptable to God as we are (warts and all), present for Love to love us. During meditation, if you find yourself listening to a thought suggesting you are doing *nothing*, gently tell it you are content to trust that God is doing *everything* – and let it go.

Whatever we might be feeling about ourselves and our prayer, rivers of living water flow within us (John 7.38). God is pouring his love into us right now, right here.

---

³ By 'ego' I don't mean the healthy activity of mind which is necessary for psychological development and functioning. In this book, 'ego' refers to the magnification of ego's activity into the drama of self-focused concern which sustains the illusion of a self that is separate from God. You might say that ego needs to be in the car to help us on our journey, just not *driving* the car.

12

'I BEGAN TO SENSE A PLACE OF PEACE AND FREEDOM'

Eve had been attending our weekly online meditation sessions for a year, but up to this point had never said anything during time for conversation. Then one day she shared something of her recent journey. 'I have a two-year-old daughter,' she began, 'and a few months before she was born, my doctor told me I have a disease that can't be cured, but only managed. The first year after the diagnosis was absolute hell. I'd look at my daughter and feel a rush of love I couldn't have imagined before she was born. And then I would be hit by a wave of sadness and fear. Sometimes I wanted to just collapse on the floor and cry until I melted away to nothing. Sometimes I felt so desperate I could have thrown myself through a window. I'd tell myself that I'd let my beautiful girl down, that I'd let my husband down, that I was a failure. I even felt guilty and a failure for feeling guilty and a failure. And when I first started coming to these meditation sessions there were plenty of moments when I wanted to shout at you!

'Then,' she continued, 'after six months of coming to the group every week and trying to practise every day, something clicked, or began to click. Trying to get rid of my sadness and fear clearly wasn't working. They didn't appear to be in any hurry to leave and the constant struggle was wearing me down. So, I decided I might as well try what I'd been hearing in the group each week. Instead of struggling with my feelings, I started to let them be present if they happened to be present. Now when they show up, I don't ignore them or fight them or beat myself up anymore. I just turn my attention to saying my prayer word and following my breath. I'm learning to sit quietly with my feelings. I'm learning to make them my place of practice.'

Eve was quiet for a few minutes, then said, 'I don't know if my sadness and fear will go away any time soon. But I know that as soon as I stopped struggling so much, my relationship with them began to change. I started to feel hope. And I began to sense a place of peace and freedom that the pain will never be able to touch.' Just before our conversation ended, she asked if I'd like to know what she calls this place within herself. I nodded and she said, 'Presence.'

Like this young mother, we can learn a new way to relate to our thoughts and our feelings. As we learn to be still and to be silent, a deeper aspect of ourselves begins to disclose itself. We begin to sense a place of peace and freedom that is always present.

13

WALKING ACROSS THE WAVES

Sometimes peace can seem a long way off, or completely hidden beneath the waves of our thoughts and feelings. Sometimes when we are finding life a challenge, it can feel as if there is no shelter from the waves crashing against us. But if we think this, we are mistaken. However large and noisy the waves may appear, there is always a refuge of peace within us.

St Diadochos likens the mind to the sea, which invites us to look into its peaceful depths when its surface is calm:

> When the sea is calm, fishermen can scan its depths and therefore hardly any creature moving in the water escapes their notice. But when the sea is disturbed by the winds it hides beneath its turbid and agitated waves what it was happy to reveal when it was smiling and calm; and then the fishermen's skill and cunning prove vain. The same thing happens with the contemplative power of the intellect.[1]

Whenever we need a refuge of peace, we can turn to the peaceful depths of awareness in which our thoughts and our feelings arise and depart. Saying our prayer word, following the flow of our breath, becoming still and quiet, we trust that God will calm the surface waves and reveal the ever-present peace that is there beneath.

---

[1] St Diadochus, *On Spiritual Knowledge*, in *The Philokalia*, Vol. 1 (London: Faber and Faber, 1983), pp. 259–60.

In the Gospel of Matthew 14.22–32, we find Jesus instructing the Disciples to make their way by boat to the other side of the lake. The dramatic sequence of events that follows provides an extraordinarily rich teaching for our practice and how to meet the challenges that waves of thoughts and feelings can present to us. In the depths of the night, at a great distance from the shore, the weather deteriorates, and the Disciples' boat starts to be tossed about, 'tormented by the waves because the wind was adverse' (14.24, DBH).[2] At this very frightening moment, Jesus comes towards them, walking on the sea. At first the disciples don't recognize him and cry out in fear. Jesus tells them who he is and that they should take heart, have courage and not be fearful. Peter says, 'Lord, if it is you, command me to come to you upon the waters' (DBH). Jesus replies, 'Come,' and Peter gets out of the boat and starts to walk towards him (Matt. 14.28–29). So far, so good.

When Peter's attention is fixed upon Jesus, when he's completely focused on responding to the invitation 'Come', he is able to do something we would not ordinarily think possible – something we might not think possible for ourselves when we are tormented by strong headwinds of adverse thoughts and feelings. He can walk across the waves. But then Peter looks away, his attention turns to the weather, and seeing the strength of the wind he starts to become afraid, and begins to sink. With his attention directed towards Jesus, Peter can walk through whatever the weather is doing. When his attention is distracted by the weather and he looks at that, he starts to sink beneath the waves. As he starts to sink, Peter cries out, 'Lord, save me!' And Jesus immediately stretches out his hand and takes hold of him, teaching him with words as if to say, 'Trust, keep your attention fixed on me, and all will be well.' They get into the boat together. The wind dies down. The lake becomes calm again.

Peace is always present in the depths of who we are.
Because this peace is who we are.

---

[2] See David Bentley Hart's evocative rendering in his translation of the New Testament (Yale University Press, 2017).

14

MEETING DIFFICULT EMOTIONS

A little while ago, someone emailed me to ask about meditation and about coping with deep, heartfelt emotions which can sometimes feel like pain, whether physical or mental. As I read their words, I remembered the many times when I've been caught up in a storm of difficult, painful emotions and struggled to be compassionate to myself, to follow Jesus' teaching, 'Be compassionate, just as your Father is compassionate' (Luke 6.36). I have seen in my own life, and in the lives of many others, how our relationship with our emotions can be transformed if we can only acknowledge what we are experiencing and learn to meet it with a spirit of self-compassion.

A way of being with difficult emotions that has been a great help to me involves a threefold movement of recognizing, allowing and feeling compassion. Recognizing what we are experiencing, we become aware of it. We can allow what we are experiencing to be present within the light of compassionate awareness. We can tend to it within this gentle light, allowing our relationship with the emotion and its energy to be transformed and peace to arise. Let's look at this a little more closely.

Recognizing

By recognizing, I mean acknowledging the emotion we are experiencing, which brings it into the light of awareness. To help us do this, we might quietly name what we are feeling, saying to ourselves, 'I am feeling sadness' or 'I am feeling anger.'

Allowing

By allowing, I mean letting the emotion we have recognized be present, simply because it is present. Saying our prayer word, following our breath, we notice and let go of any thoughts, any mind-chatter about the emotion we are experiencing, and we allow the experience to be present, naked and just as it is. We drop any inclination to avoid or fix anything, and allow what is here to just be here, practising Jesus' teaching not to let ourselves be caught up in worries about tomorrow, or in what we did or didn't do yesterday, or 20 years ago (Matt. 6.34). We allow what we are experiencing to be our meditation seat, our place of practice. If we need a little help with this (we all do), we can return to quietly recognizing and naming what we are experiencing ('I am feeling sadness', 'I am feeling anger') as many times as we need to. It's always good to recognize and allow the simple reality of our experience in the present moment. Then we return to our practice, to saying our prayer word, following our breath, trusting that God, the ground of all compassion, is present and ready to comfort us, to bear our burden and give us rest, even as the emotion, the pain, is present (2 Cor. 1.3; Matt. 11.28).

Compassion

One of the great gifts of our practice is how the stilling of the reactive, chattering mind clears a space for compassion to arise. In the moment of recognition, allowing what is present in our experience to be present, compassion arises quite naturally to meet our suffering. In the calm space of awareness, we can recognize our experience, our pain, our anger. We can allow what is present to be present and we can tend to it with the gentle light of compassion. We can allow self-compassion. We can allow ourselves to be embraced by others and receive their compassion. We can allow our relationship with the emotion and its energy to be transformed, and allow peace to arise.

Many years ago, when I was 20, going through a difficult time and desperately needing a ray of light, my teacher said to me, 'Chris, whatever you are feeling or thinking right now, try not to forget that

God is not just within you, but is ceaselessly manifesting as you. We are *Compassion, compassioning*; we are *Love, loving*. This is who we are.' Our most heartfelt emotions, which can sometimes feel like physical or mental pain, run deep. But they do not run as deep as we do. In our depths there is only love, only peace, only compassion, even as the storm is bearing down on us. The compassion we touch in meditation is God's ceaseless gift of himself to us, a single movement of love, an ever-present embrace.

15

'I'M JUST AN ANXIOUS PERSON'

Learning to greet our thoughts and feelings with stillness and silence, instead of immediately filling our heads with a story about them, can offer us a powerful sense of liberation and the possibility for radical change in our lives. As we learn to see beyond what we tell ourselves about ourselves, the boundaries of our mental and emotional world begin to open and dissolve, and the simple truth of our life unfolds ever more clearly and brightly.

William is a brilliant teacher. His students and colleagues respect and like him in equal measure. But despite being well-liked and admired, William had long suffered frequent bouts of anxiety and recurrent painful thoughts. Sometimes the anxiety would appear like a grey presence in the background of the day, noticeable but manageable. At other times (and all too frequently), the anxiety seemed to swell and overshadow every moment, tightening its grip until William found it a struggle even to be awake. For reasons linked to a dramatic incident in his early life, even the smallest feeling of anxiety could serve as a trigger for William, a trigger to begin weaving a fearful story around that feeling. Most often, the story he told himself would begin with making some sort of small mistake, then steadily growing to the proportions of a small disaster, resulting in his colleagues (and pretty much the whole world) discovering that he was not an excellent teacher after all, but incompetent and a failure. Sometimes the story would be about how he was fundamentally weak and deeply selfish, and that sooner or later (in suitably dramatic circumstances), people would come to see this and to reject him, leaving him to spend his life feeling even more lonely than he often did. For almost 45 years, William had told himself and others, 'I'm just an anxious person,' assuming this was who he was and how his life would always be. This was where William began his practice of meditation. And so it came as quite a shock (though a hope-filled one) to have it gently suggested to him that the painful stories he had been telling himself about himself in reality bore no relation at all to the extraordinary truth of his deepest identity.

Practising meditation each day, William learned to greet his anxious thoughts and feelings with increasing stillness, to let them simply be there if they happened to be present, and to release any story he might be telling himself about them by quietly lifting his attention off the story and returning it to his practice. Steadily but surely, like a spring slowly soaking the soil of his life (Isa. 35.7), William began to discover a place of inner peace and stability he had never known before. And as he continued with his practice, his sense of this inner peace and stability continued to deepen and quietly reveal its foundation in the silent depths of God.

Initial thoughts and feelings will always do what they do, arising as naturally as clouds in the sky, manifesting in different forms for each of us. (We are all complex amalgams of biology, personal history and conditioning.) What we come to see in meditation is that these initial thoughts or feelings, minus the stories we tell ourselves in reaction to them, are just simple thoughts and feelings. William came to realize that he couldn't avoid pain in his life, but that he could learn to notice and pause the stories he told himself *about* the pain. It is largely the stories we tell ourselves that we experience as suffering. As we learn to observe thoughts and feelings with greater stillness and less comment, the noisy walls we erect between ourselves and those around us and life are gently dismantled, brick by brick.

Little by little, as William learned to greet his life from a quieter foothold, he became increasingly aware that his thoughts and feelings arose and departed within a peaceful spaciousness, and began to encounter his life and those around him in a completely new light. He realized that if he could look at a thought or feeling, he couldn't *be* that thought or feeling, because he was the one looking. And so he began to ponder a question of great significance: 'What do I look like?' One day, when William was sitting quietly, he saw that even as anxiety was present, he was not anxious, that anxiety had no place in the depths of his identity. He realized that whatever he might have to face in the future, he could not be harmed by mental and emotional noise and turmoil, any more than the ocean can be harmed by the waves that move on its surface, or the sky by the weather that passes through it.

In her work *The Revelations (or Showings) of Divine Love*, Julian of Norwich writes, 'For I saw very clearly that where our Lord appears, peace reigns, and anger has no place; for I saw no kind of anger in God.'[1] The Lord 'appears' in the deepest truth of who we are, *as* that deepest truth. What does this truth look like? Language fails us as we behold these depthless depths. All William could say was, 'Awareness, light-filled awareness. Depthless peace.'

We are not our thoughts and feelings.
*We are where they **happen**.*

---

[1] Julian of Norwich, *Revelations of Divine Love*, trans. Barry Windeatt (Oxford: Oxford University Press, 2015), Chapter 49, p. 103.

16

TAMING OUR INNER CRITIC

Like me, you may have gone through childhood thinking you needed to contain or suppress strong feelings, that to express them might not be acceptable. Or you may have been raised in a church that said (or left you with a concern) that certain feelings are wrong. One way or another, many people come to believe that what they feel is unacceptable, that experiencing certain strong feelings means some part of *themselves* might be unacceptable. With the practice of meditation, we can gradually learn to meet our feelings, to meet what we might have feared is unacceptable in ourselves.

When we can *acknowledge*, *name* and *allow* our feelings – the sadness, the shame, the heat of anger, the heartbreak of grief, as well as the delights of pleasure and the intoxicating depths of joy – just as they are, minus the stories we tell ourselves about ourselves in *reaction* to them, we enter a process of great liberation. Next comes the freedom to *express* our feelings. Not in a way that might simply be throwing our hurt or anger at someone else, but in finding we can say, 'This is how I feel. This is what is important to me. This is what I need.' Connecting with our feelings like this helps us to reconnect with others, to be more fully, authentically present in our relationships.

If for whatever reason we had to suppress our childhood feelings, to express our fear, our anger, our hurt or frustration, can be very scary at first. The critic we internalized is likely to appear and have plenty to say, spinning all manner of accusations in our heads and rehearsing a variety of fearful stories about being told off or shamed, about being disliked or rejected. If we come from a background where anger and frustration, demands and conflicts were frequently flying around or barely contained, we might be afraid that expressing our feelings may release a destructive storm, overwhelming us or others. The wisdom and healing processes of meditation can help us meet and give voice to our feelings. The simple practice helps integrate and harmonize all dimensions of our being, and opens us to a freedom and peace we might never have imagined.

In the Parable of the Weeds among the Wheat, we hear Jesus teaching that the field of our life contains seeds that grow into wheat and seeds that grow into weeds, and that we shouldn't be too quick to try and pull up the weeds (Matt. 13.24–30). In fact, Jesus says very directly that we *shouldn't* pull them up, that we should allow the wheat and weeds to grow together. The weeds have a role to play. Met with greater silence and less reactivity, the weeds can become invaluable doorways, opportunities to practise and discover greater awareness, freedom and compassion. When we meditate, we learn to be fully present in the field of our life. We learn to sit with the wheat *and* the weeds. Our practice is not to try and weed out what we would prefer not to see, but to cultivate a wholly new relationship with all that we encounter. Sitting silently with what we dislike, with what we dislike in ourselves (or have been taught to dislike), can teach us a great deal.

It's perfectly natural for all sorts of thoughts to arise during our time of practice, and we are likely to notice them with much greater clarity. As we bring our whole attention to the gentle repetition of our prayer word (or short phrase) in union with the flow of our breath, the surface mind stills and awareness opens. Remember how St Diadochos compares the mind to the sea and says how when it is calm (less agitated with thoughts and chatter) we can look deeply within. When wheat-like thoughts appear, many of us will be glad to welcome them and to feel pleased with ourselves. When weed-like thoughts appear, many of us might feel disappointed with ourselves, or a great deal worse than that. But our practice remains exactly the same, whether we like what we see or not. We greet all that arises within us with silence and quietly return to our practice.

Speaking from her own deep experience of contending with thoughts, St Teresa of Avila notes, 'The harder you try *not* to think of anything, the *more* aroused your mind will become and you will think even more.'¹ Trying not to have thoughts or feelings doesn't work. If we say to ourselves 'I will not have a thought,' we've just added another thought to the pile! Trying to battle directly with thoughts proves equally unhelpful and frustrating. If we think we can uproot an unwelcome thought through sheer head-on force of will, we quickly discover that all we have been doing is watering and feeding it with our attention, helping it grow larger, more stubborn and more persistent. However frustrating or painful they may be, each of our weed-like thoughts brings an opportunity. Instead of automatically reacting to them with fear or self-reproach, we can choose to see them as invitations to practise: to practise patience and understanding, to practise being compassionate, just as our Father is compassionate (Luke 6.36).

After silencing the crowd of accusers by means of his silence, Jesus said to the woman who was about to be stoned, '"Where are they? Does no one condemn you?" And she said, "No one, Lord." And Jesus said, "Neither do I"' (John 8.1–11, DBH). Just as Jesus silenced the accusers by means of his silence, Christ helps us silence the accusing voices within ourselves by means of our deepening silence. Greeting thoughts with silence, we avoid getting caught up in judgemental thoughts about our thoughts, which is to say we avoid getting caught up in judgemental thoughts about ourselves. We learn to greet ourselves with quiet compassion. We discover, like the woman who was about to be stoned, that there is no one judging us, there is no one condemning us.

'One of the most important insights that comes from working with silence,' writes the Anglican solitary Maggie Ross, 'is that nothing in our lives is wasted.'² Even the most difficult weeds, the most painful realities of our life, can become gifts that enrich the soil of our practice and help reveal the treasure buried in the field of our life. Patterns and habits of thought may run deep, but they do not run as deep as we do. In our depths there is only infinite, unconditional, unalterable love, the love we call God.

---

[1] St Teresa of Avila, *The Interior Castle*, trans. Miribai Starr (New York: Riverhead Books, 2003), p. 107 (emphasis added).

[2] Maggie Ross, *Silence: A User's Guide, Volume 1: Process* (London: Darton, Longman and Todd, 2014), p. 24.

17

TRANSFORMING OUR FEAR

'In childhood,' writes the poet Jane Hirshfield,

> great happiness and profound grief run close to the surface. Adult life tamps these flarings of feeling down, so that practical tasks might be done. My poems in recent years have sought increasingly to notice joy, not least because, as the world has darkened, I've needed joy's restorative counterweight. But the poems have also increasingly opened to grief, bewilderment, even to fear. The poems want – I want – to become the trembling compass of a full human life.[1]

In everyday life, when a difficult thought or feeling arises, we can quickly try to push it away or cover it up. But in meditation we allow what is difficult to be here if it happens to be here. The awareness we cultivate helps us acknowledge our fear or our pain, and greet it in a way that can immediately bring some relief and peace. We notice its presence. We don't struggle with it. If we know how to greet what we find difficult, we reduce our suffering and we need not be afraid of being overwhelmed. Quietly acknowledging what we find difficult, without resistance, without struggle, we discover that our relationship with fear is transformed.

Katy, a talented senior leader in local government, has built a strong reputation in her field of expertise, and is a regular contributor

---

[1] Jane Clark and Barbara Vellacott, 'Poetry in the Contemporary World: Conversations with Jane Hirshfield', *Beshara Magazine*, 20 (2002), https://besharamagazine.org/arts-literature/jane-hirshfield-poetry-conversation/, accessed 19.03.2025.

to specialist publications and a popular keynote speaker at conferences. The arrival of Covid-19 and national lockdowns meant not just cancelled conferences and a switch to largely working from home, but triggered the onset of frequent fearful thoughts, which occasionally coalesced into bouts of debilitating anxiety. As soon as an initial fearful thought arose, her mind would grasp hold of it and produce a stream of fearful reactive thoughts: 'Why has this happened to me?' 'Why am I so stupidly weak!?' As so often happens, Katy's reactive thoughts seemed to intensify and grow louder in the dark, quiet hours of the night: 'This is getting worse and worse!' 'I might lose my job, my house and everything I love!'

Up to this point, Katy's familiarity with meditation extended to a breathing exercise after yoga classes and a light body-scan during the occasional well-being session on holiday. Now Katy's spiritual well-being became a central concern to her. She attended an introductory meditation retreat, started going to a weekly group, established a daily practice, and quickly came to see how she was creating mental suffering for herself. 'It's like when you wake up in the night and want to go back to sleep,' she said. 'You start thinking about going to sleep, then about how you're *not* going to sleep, then about how *not* sleeping is going to ruin your day – all of which is pretty much guaranteed to keep you awake!'

Katy recognized the difference between an initial thought or feeling and the tortuous reactive commentaries she routinely wrapped around them and trapped herself within. 'I realized there was little I could do to stop the first scary thought coming into my mind, but that there was a great deal I could do to change my relationship with it. I suddenly saw how I'd been torturing myself, that filling my mind with all sorts of fearful thoughts *about* fear was far worse than the initial fearful thought or feeling!' In a remarkably short time, Katy learned a great deal about how to greet a fearful thought or feeling with compassionate stillness; how, through simply noticing their presence and turning her attention to saying her prayer word and her breath, she could come home to a place that is always peaceful, always available, and rest there.

Quietly acknowledging what we find difficult, without struggle, allows our relationship with fear to be transformed. In the words of

Martin Laird, 'Whatever it is in us that grasps and craves is soothed and calmed and begins to loosen its grip.'[2] In practical terms, this may mean falling asleep with more ease, surprising ourselves at how well we led that terrifying meeting or enjoying that coffee with someone we had put off seeing for weeks. We discover ourselves becoming more present, more available for the gift of our life in ways we might never have expected. Greeting each moment with simple awareness, we clear a space for peace and joy to arise within 'the trembling compass of a full human life.'[3]

---

[2] Martin Laird, *A Sunlit Absence: Silence, Awareness and Contemplation* (Oxford: Oxford University Press, 2011), p. 72.

[3] Clark and Vellacott, 'Poetry in the Contemporary World'.

18

STOP JUDGING YOUR PRACTICE

One of the earliest obstacles we have to overcome in meditation is the temptation to try and judge our practice. In the wonderful Napoleonic-era novels of Patrick O'Brian, the crews on Captain Aubrey's ships had a very clear idea of what *real* medicine should taste like. Swallowing something absolutely vile was very reassuring. Dr Stephen Maturin, the ship's physician, quickly learned to add something vile-tasting to whatever medicine he prepared. Even if the therapeutic benefits of a medicine were limited, its vileness was considered strong evidence that here was a physician who really knew his stuff, and morale was duly raised.

Many come to meditation carrying strong ideas of how it should look and feel and 'taste'. When it doesn't appear like this, they can quickly begin trying to judge their practice, which in addition to being bad for morale is impossible.

One of the common myths about meditation is that good practice will somehow whisk away the quirks of our character, magically remove what we don't like about ourselves and help sort out the life issues we would rather not face. It's quite understandable to bring such ideas to meditation at first. The covers of many glossy meditation magazines seem to suggest that good practice looks like a blissed-out smile, flawless skin, and a tendency to spend your spare time sitting in a full lotus posture in a beautiful meadow, surrounded by flowers and adoring animals. But good practice doesn't remove our life issues or mean that we are never short-tempered. The enlightened person still feel uncomfortable when they've eaten too much rich food, and pain when they stub their toe.

The healing processes of meditation take place in silence at the deepest level of our being, largely out of sight. We can make no judgement about them. Each time we practise, we commit ourselves to a future we cannot see or know, so faith (trust) is essential. You might have noticed that when healing miracles happen in the Gospels, Jesus doesn't say, 'I healed you,' but 'Your faith has made you whole.' The Evangelists tell us that Jesus was afraid that people would clutch hold of what they could see and feel, and would overlook what these signs point to – our infinite potential to realize our oneness with God and to grow into God's likeness as bearers of his love in the world.

A great many people when they first come to meditation find it a challenge to let go of a particularly unhelpful picture of what good practice looks like: *no* thoughts, *no* distractedness. Despite hearing it said very clearly that meditation is *not* about not having thoughts, but about changing our *relationship* with our thoughts, it's very common for someone to say (and I suspect most of us will have said this to ourselves), 'I don't think it went well. I had dozens of thoughts, one after another.' The subsequent conversation with a good teacher often runs like this: 'So, you saw dozens of thoughts?' 'Yes.' 'And each time you noticed you were noticing these thoughts you returned your attention to your practice?' 'Yes.' 'So, you had dozens of moments of awareness?' 'I guess so. Yes.' 'Why do you think your meditation didn't go well?' This last question is usually greeted with a smile, because the penny has dropped.

People usually do perfectly well with their practice, right from the beginning. What our practice *looks* or *feels* like to us during our time of meditation is not the point. The point of meditation is the whole of our life. This is where the healing and gifts of our practice manifest. Will there be signs of our practice going well? Yes, there will be. But it's very likely that others will notice the fruits of our practice before we do. They may notice that we are a little calmer, a little slower to react in certain ways. They might notice that we are a little more peaceful, patient and loving. We won't suddenly find ourselves having no troublesome thoughts to deal with. Our gradual healing and enlightenment are the gradual process of our integration into the pristine truth of who we are. God doesn't want us to be something like a contemplative Marvel hero, but human. What does this look like? It looks like Christ. It looks like love, solidarity and friendship.

All we need do is begin. And keep beginning. We do not need to worry. We do not need to struggle. What we seek is closer to us than we are to ourselves. And we have been given all we need for the journey.

19

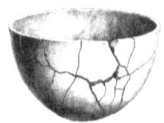

'THERE'S A CRACK IN EVERYTHING'

Ring the bells that still can ring
Forget your perfect offering
There is a crack, a crack in everything
That's how the light gets in.[1]

Leonard Cohen's striking lyrics help remind us that we don't need to escape from our humanness in order to find healing and enlightenment. Quite the opposite. God in Christ meets us in our brokenness, in our failures and our wounds, and transforms them into doorways of light. The path of meditation does not lead us *away* from the vulnerabilities of the human condition, but helps illuminate and guide us *through* them. It is often those who have suffered most, who have met, befriended and lived the truth of their vulnerability, who have a special gift for meditation, who sense most clearly the depthless love which knows and holds all our wounds.

Some people come to meditation thinking (or hoping) that the practice can be used to look away from their wounds, that if they can bury themselves in their practice they might be able to avoid seeing what they would rather not see and avoid meeting what they need to meet. Occasionally people think they have failed in their practice when, after meditating faithfully for some time, they discover that they are still who they are, carrying the same vulnerabilities. But they haven't failed at all. They have succeeded in meeting themselves. They

---

[1] Leonard Cohen, 'Anthem', *The Future*, Columbia Records, 1992.

may have failed to hold on to a false picture of what the spiritual life is about, but they have crossed an essential threshold on their journey into love – to knowing that they are loved just as they are. One of the seeming paradoxes of meditation is how the indescribable healing and peace we discover come to us through our wounds and vulnerability. For many people, this breaking through of grace can feel at first like a breaking down, a deconstruction of so much they had believed about themselves and the spiritual journey. What is in every sense a receiving involves a letting go, a releasing.

Most of us, to one extent or another, are deeply conditioned to hide from our vulnerabilities and brokenness. Faced with pain and apparent failure, we routinely tell ourselves painful stories about ourselves, feeding deep feelings of shame. All too quickly, we judge ourselves for simply being human. But it is precisely in our humanness, our vulnerability, our woundedness, that we are shown how God enfolds and encloses us in his infinite loving embrace. And it is at these points of pain and self-judgement that the support of a loving practice community is invaluable. Whatever we might be experiencing in our life, we can choose to grow just where we are planted. We can say 'yes' to the subtle invitation in our hearts to open within the ever-present presence of God.

A few years ago, someone emailed to tell me how meditation was helping her find a completely different relationship with her life. She wrote: 'I was scared when I first came to meditation. I was longing for peace and something inside me recognized the wisdom of the practice, but I was scared of being overwhelmed if I stopped running and let everything catch up with me. I've spent years carrying a lot of emotional pain. And in order to try and cope, I filled my life with all sorts of activity and busyness.

'I've finally seen that I don't need to run, that I can just be here. Life's still not easy sometimes, but I know I am free. I am free to meet what I need to meet with more wisdom and compassion. If pain is here, I can just be with it, without judging, without judging myself. To finally have moments of stillness, of peace, to simply be present in the present, is so wonderful. I don't know how to put this, but somehow, even in moments of pain, I know that the deepest part of who I am is love, and that this love is loving me. I still have baggage. But I no longer feel that I'm carrying it alone. I have the sense that *I'm* being carried.'

We are not healed through getting rid of our wounds, or in spite of them, but *through* them. As we've heard Maggie Ross say,

> In Christian theology nothing is wasted, nothing is left behind; through wounds comes healing. In the resurrection, the wounds of Christ do not disappear; they are glorified. The desert solitaries tell us that only the devil [ignorance, misperception] disguising himself as Christ has no wounds, being too vain to bear them.[2]

The path of meditation teaches us how to meet our wounds with compassion and without judgement. Learning to accept and indwell our vulnerability, we discover a place of deep communion, a place of solidarity and compassion for all in the silent ground of our shared humanity.

> *Ring the bells that still can ring*
> *Forget your perfect offering*
> *There is a crack, a crack in everything*
> *That's how the light gets in.*

---

[2] Maggie Ross, *Silence: A User's Guide, Volume 1: Process* (London: Darton, Longman and Todd, 2014), p. 98.

20

FLOWERS IN THE DESERT

If boredom becomes an occasional or even a regular companion during our practice, that may be a very good thing. The experience of boredom (sometimes called 'dryness' by teachers of prayer) is often an indication that we have come to an important doorway and are already passing over its threshold. The deepening of prayer most often appears to our senses like a featureless desert, because sooner or later, our practice is deepening beyond what our senses can grasp.

As for Jesus, our prayer is purified in the desert. And ego doesn't like the desert at all. It will try to coax you to do anything other than sitting still in this featureless place. Ego is constantly looking for something to grasp onto and entertain itself with. It might suggest you put on some soothing 'ambient' music; or light another candle; or that you may gain much more spiritual benefit by reading this or that book; and of course, it would be quite wrong (ungrateful, even) to ignore that wonderful holy thought that just appeared in your head! And if all that fails, ego may suggest, part-way through your practice, that you might consider changing your prayer word to one that is more obviously spiritual and meaningful. Anything, really, to stop you quietly sitting in the desert and refusing to entertain it. But remarkable things happen in the desert. The desert is a womb of grace, bearing the most extraordinary gift for those who can wait patiently for its featureless wrapping to unfurl. If we are content to follow the path of meditation beyond the demands of ego, beyond what our senses can grasp, what has hitherto been experienced as an empty, boring place begins to reveal its infinite fullness.

Speaking of the return to Zion (the return to the deepest truth of who we are), Isaiah compares the blossoming of awareness to a bursting forth of life in the desert (Isa. 35). The Prophet's song tells of how the wilderness will be glad, how the desert will rejoice and the ground will bloom and burst into flower – of how we will be healed and made whole as streams of life-giving water pour upon the parched land and make it green. And how a highway will be found there, called the Holy Way.

The path of meditation takes us on an unusual journey. Unlike most journeys we've ever been on, this path requires us to throw away our luggage, our clothes, everything that might distract us. Content to simply be still and quiet, we trust that the desert will blossom in its own good time. We're not going anywhere. We're coming home.

21

WALKING BY FAITH, NOT BY SIGHT

A great deal of talk about the 'spiritual life' seems to suggest that the best proof of being on the right 'spiritual track' is to be found in certain tangible experiences. This is hardly surprising. Our culture idolizes experience. Retailers offer us *retail experiences*. Food producers offer us *food experiences*. And more than a few churches offer us *worship experiences*, or the possibility of an *experience* of the Spirit. It couldn't be more different with meditation in the Christian tradition. One of the first things we learn is to stop looking for any sort of experience. 'Whenever you feel yourself drawn to this work of contemplation,' says the author of *The Cloud of Unknowing*, 'a naked intent directed to God is fully sufficient.'[1] As we have heard St John of the Cross say, it is enough to 'preserve a loving attentiveness to God, with no desire to feel or understand any particular thing concerning him.'[2] Rather than looking for anything to happen, we open ourselves to what is always happening. We turn to that which is so close, so intimate, that to *look* for it is to *overlook* it.

The path of meditation is a path of self-forgetfulness, a path which teaches us to trust, 'for we walk by faith, not by sight' (2 Cor. 5.7, NAB). For God to *increase* in our awareness, we must *decrease* (John 3.30). Letting go of any desire for 'signs and wonders' (John 4.48, NRSVUK), we come to see that everything is a sign, that life itself

---

[1] Translated from the Middle English edition of *The Cloud of Unknowing and The Book of Privy Counselling*, edited by Phyllis Hodgson (Oxford: Oxford University Press for the Early English Text Society, 1981), p. 28.

[2] *The Collected Works of St John of the Cross*, trans. Kieran Kavanaugh and Otilio Rodriguez (Washington DC: Institute of Carmelite Studies, 1991), p. 92.

is a wonder. As Rowan Williams so beautifully put it, we come to see that 'Creation around you, within you, the creation that you are, the creation you are part of, is all God acting, God loving, God inviting, here and now.'[3] However surprising this way of prayer might seem at first, we soon discover the great wisdom and peace to be found in simply saying our prayer word and following our breath.

In a sermon called 'The Nobleman', the great fourteenth-century Dominican Meister Eckhart gives a teaching on self-forgetfulness which is of great value for the practice of meditation.[4] In characteristic fashion (a blend of profound wisdom, bracing clarity, and playfulness), Eckhart notes how some people think that 'the flower and kernel of bliss' is to be found in *knowing* that we see and know God. He asks, 'For if I had all joy and did not know it, what good would that be to me, and what joy would that be?' And immediately answers, 'But I definitely deny that it is so.'

Eckhart is not saying that the self-conscious knowing of experience is 'bad'. Quite the opposite. Indeed, he says we cannot be happy without it. Experience is essential for understanding and living in the world. What Eckhart says is that our happiness does not depend on it. Experience is always an act of interpretation, a re-presentation to ourselves of what we encounter, and in that sense, one step removed. 'The first condition of happiness', Eckhart says,

> is that the soul [awareness] sees God naked [without being clothed in our ideas and concepts]. From that she derives all her being and her life, and draws all that she is, from the ground of God, knowing nothing of knowledge, nor of love, nor of anything at all. She is utterly calm in God's being, knowing nothing but being there and God. But when she is [self-consciously] aware and *knows* that she sees, knows, and loves God, that is a turning away …

---

[3] Premier Unbelievable?, 'Rowan Williams & Paul Kingsnorth: Conversion, Culture, and the Cross', *YouTube*, 3 June 2022, https://www.youtube.com/watch?v=iCxznkRKa1w, accessed 19.03.2025.

[4] See 'The Nobleman' in *The Complete Mystical Works of Meister Eckhart*, trans. M. Walshe (New York: Crossroads, 2009), pp. 557–64 (translation altered slightly, emphasis added).

If any of this might sound a little strange, we can look at our ordinary experience of listening to music or reading a novel to help us understand what Eckhart is talking about. When we are 'lost' in a piece of beautiful music or a wonderful novel, there is no sense of separation, no self-conscious self sitting here listening or reading to be found. We become one with the music, one with the novel. We are most definitely present – but enjoying a particular quality of presentness we might call *boundless awareness*. It has no borders, no edges. It is all-encompassing. But when we *know* we are listening or *know* we are reading, this self-conscious knowing is what Eckhart calls 'a turning away'. When we turn towards the content of our experience, the sense of a separate self arises, that there is someone here experiencing a separate something.

For Eckhart, the ultimate ground of our happiness and peace is not to be found in self-consciousness but in *self-forgetfulness*, a losing of ourselves in God and a losing of God in ourselves – a losing which is a finding, a going out from ourselves which is a coming home within God: 'Therefore, our Lord says in very truth that eternal life is knowing God alone as true God, and not in [self-consciously] *knowing* that one knows God (John 17.3).'

Letting go of any desire to find God in experience, we come to rest in God who has found us from eternity. Letting go of ourselves, all that remains is 'God acting, God loving, God inviting, here and now.'

Part Three

BECOMING PLACES OF PEACE

God is not hiding. You are.
He's ready for you, waits with
infinite patience.

22

BEING WITH GOD WITHOUT ANY AGENDA

The seemingly relentless pressure to be conspicuously 'doing' and 'performing' in our daily life can very easily carry over into how we approach meditation. Many of us will have been taught to think of prayer as something we do, towards God, for God, another thing on the list of things we must 'perform' to be in the right place with God. But this is a misunderstanding, a symptom of the heavy yoke of self-justification, an unnecessary burden that Jesus teaches us to put down (Matt. 11.28–30). To paraphrase St Paul, we do not know how to pray as we ought, and we don't need to, because the Spirit prays on our behalf (Rom. 8.26–27). 'Now that seems to me an enormously encouraging remark,' says the Dominican Herbert McCabe.

> It is encouraging because it is quite common for someone to feel that she or he personally is the only one who doesn't know how to pray. Well, at least we have one of the greatest saints in history with us. Paul too did not know how to pray. But notice that he didn't expect to ...[1]

God is the ground of our prayer, the ground from which our prayers arise and in which all prayer is rooted. There are many ways to pray, and we will all pray in different ways at different times; but ultimately these are all ways for us to participate in what *God* is doing, which is nothing other than ceaselessly giving us the gift of himself

---

[1] Herbert McCabe OP, *God Still Matters* (London: Continuum, 2002), p. 215.

as the Life of our life. In meditation, our practice is to be with God without any agenda. We just sit, as we are, where we are. We rest from thinking about God, and we allow ourselves to be with him. We rest from thinking about our life, and we allow ourselves to more fully inhabit it. To *be* with God it is not necessary to fill our mind with thoughts *about* God, not even one. Our way to realizing our foundational oneness with God is not by thinking, but by releasing every thought that obscures this simple truth. To begin our journey to the depths of this oneness, advises the author of *The Cloud of Unknowing*, it is enough to simply lift up our hearts 'with a humble stirring of love.' No thoughts are needed, 'for a naked intention directed to God is fully sufficient, without any other goal than himself.'[2]

A schoolteacher friend told me how she had found peace in the simplicity of meditation. 'At first,' she said, 'each time I sat to meditate my head would fill with thoughts about whether I was doing it right. After several weeks of this, I woke up one night and it struck me: I wasn't just worried about not being good enough at meditation, I was worried about not being good enough at anything, I was worried about not being good enough at Life.' After a few minutes of silence, she continued, 'Then I remembered Jesus' words, "Come to me, all who toil and are burdened, and I shall give you rest", and I decided to trust this. The next time I practised, I looked at these words for a few minutes before I began. I realized that I could simply be here, just as I am; that I could let go of my burden of worries and rest in God, without having to do anything in particular. I can't explain it. And I don't mind not being able to. It's a little like stepping into a vast, gentle river. I let my worries go, lift up my feet and lie back in the water, trusting it will support me. When I meditate now, I don't think about what I need to do, or where I want to go. I'm quite happy to rest there, and let the river carry me wherever it wants to go.'

---

[2] *The Cloud of Unknowing and Other Works*, trans. A. C. Spearing (London: Penguin Books, 2001), p. 29.

23

THE OPPORTUNITY OF OUR LIFE

'Just practise living peacefully with your ordinary life. Begin afresh each day, each hour, each moment.' I don't mind admitting feeling a certain disappointment when one of my first and most important teachers, the Benedictine monk Sylvester Houédard, suggested I stop dreaming about enlightenment.[1] I had recently come to live at Prinknash Abbey, and came away from our conversation very determined to follow his advice – and immediately replaced my pictures of enlightenment with some rather romantic pictures about what living peacefully with my ordinary life would look like. When Sylvester asked me a couple of weeks later how things were going, I instantly knew he had seen straight through what I was doing. He patiently encouraged me to let go of my latest glossy notions of what the spiritual life was all about.

In meditation we practise living peacefully with each moment. We simply say our word and follow our breath, greeting each moment without any idea of what that moment should look like or feel like. It goes without saying that this is easier said than done. As we've already noted, most of us come to meditation with some idea of how we want our meditation to look and feel, which is to say how we want our life to look and feel; hence my teacher's advice to let this go and just begin, and begin, and keep beginning. In the stillness of meditation, we become aware of our desires and preferences for all sorts of things. We see the subtle ways we try to avoid being with

---

[1] Beshara Publications, 'Dom Sylvester Houédard', *Beshara Publications*, n.d., https://besharapublications.org.uk/dom-sylvester-houedard/, accessed 19.03.2025.

the reality of our life. We come face to face with our fears, with our resistance to meeting ourselves and simply being who we are. Which is why practice sometimes takes courage. It takes courage to just be still. It takes courage to stop reacting to life the way we've always done; to pause, to see, to do something entirely different. We need to show ourselves kindness. And we benefit greatly from the loving support of others, as in our practice community.[2] This teaching from the time of the Desert Fathers and Mothers is full of wise advice and gentle encouragement for all of us:

> A brother went through a time of such a struggle that he couldn't keep his monastic rule. Later, when he tried to start keeping even the basics of the rule, he was hampered by his suffering. He said to himself, 'When will I be as I used to be?' In this gloomy state of mind, he could not even bring himself to start his prayers. In great despair, he sought guidance from a hermit and told him what had been happening. When the hermit heard of his sufferings, he told him this story by way of example: A man had a plot of land, which he neglected. In his carelessness brambles sprang up and it became a wilderness of thistles and thorns. Then he decided to cultivate it and he said to his son, 'Go and clear that ground.' So, the son went to clear it, and saw that the thistles and thorns had multiplied. And his resolve weakened, and he said, 'It's going to take an endless amount of time to clear and weed all this.' He was so overwhelmed that he lay down and went to sleep. And he did this day after day. When his father came to see what he had done he found him doing nothing and said to him, 'Why have you done nothing till now?' The boy said to his father, 'I was coming to work, Father, but when I saw this wilderness of thorn and thistle I was overwhelmed and too intimidated to start, and so I lay on the ground and went to sleep.' Then his father said to him, 'Son, if you had cleared a little each day, even the area on which you lay down, your work would have

---

[2] 'Meditation in the Christian Tradition', The School of Contemplative Life, https://schoolofcontemplativelife.com/meditation-in-the-christian-tradition/, accessed 28.03.2025.

advanced slowly and you would not have lost heart.' So the boy followed his father's advice and in a short time the land was cultivated. The hermit added, 'So, Brother, just do a little work and do not be discouraged, and God will give you grace and bring you back to your proper way of life.' The brother went away and patiently did what the hermit had told him. And doing so, he found peace of mind, and made progress with the help of the Lord Christ.[3]

In meditation, we stop listening to the discriminating mind that is only too happy to chatter until the cows come home about how life really *ought* to be looking or feeling. Letting go of the thought that a sound is annoying, we discover that there is just the experience of sound, which is neither good nor bad. Letting go of our thoughts about the presence of pain or fear, there is just the experience of pain or fear, which is more than enough to deal with. When the discriminating mind isn't present, life continues just as it is, but our *experience* of life becomes more open, flexible and peaceful. Instead of experiencing ourselves as someone opposing this or that aspect of life, we are more able to move with life's movement, to flow with life's flow. The problems of life don't suddenly stop. Life continues with its habit of happening. But our whole relationship with life has changed. Sooner or later, we begin to see that beneath all the mental and emotional noise and turmoil we face in life is a depthless depth of peace which is always present.

---

[3] *The Desert Fathers: Sayings of the Early Christian Monks* (London: Penguin Classics, 2003), Chapter 7 (Fortitude), Saying 40 (slightly altered).

24

ENLIGHTENMENT IN EVERYDAY LIFE

With great gentleness, my teachers at Prinknash Abbey encouraged me to stop looking for enlightenment (the kingdom) as if this were something separate from ordinary daily life lived with a particular quality of open, receptive attention. Whatever task I happened to be doing, which included a great deal of time working in the kitchen and gardens, cleaning toilets and polishing endless wooden floors, I was to practise bringing a quality of awareness to it, to be as wholeheartedly present as possible. I was being encouraged to let go of any notion that the so-called 'spiritual life' was something distinct from the most mundane aspects of our everyday life, lived together.

A philosopher once asked the Buddha what his monks do all day. The Buddha answered that they walk, stand, sit, lie down, wash their bowls and clean. Puzzled by this, the philosopher asked how the monks' lives were any different from anyone else's. The Buddha replied that when they walk, they walk. When they stand, they stand. When they sit, they sit. When they lie down, they lie down. And when they wash their bowls and clean, they wash their bowls and clean. I'm not sure how far the Buddha's answer satisfied the philosopher, but the Buddha was saying that the practice of the monks is simply to be fully present for what needs tending to, to be present, moment by moment, for the gift of their life.

When Jesus was asked when the kingdom of God would come (as if it were something separate from us and might appear at some point in the future), he answered, 'The coming of the kingdom cannot be observed, and no one will announce, "Behold! here it is", or,

"Behold! there it is." For behold! the kingdom of God is within you' (Luke 17.20–21). It's easy to overlook the astonishing invitation, as well as its challenge: behold (see), the kingdom cannot be observed by the thinking mind, because the kingdom is the boundless awareness within which the thinking mind arises (the mind that looks for the kingdom is like a wave that looks for the ocean). The kingdom is not going to come, because it's already here, within all of us. Every question *about* the kingdom arises *within* it. The important question, the *life-changing* question, is not, 'When is the kingdom going to be present for us?' but, 'When are we going to be present for the kingdom – the kingdom which is the gift of contemplation, of seeing clearly, of transfigured awareness?' We receive this gift, says St Isaac the Syrian, when 'our mind has been freed from its many conceptions and enters the unified simplicity of purity [of oneness] … and becomes as a little child.'[1] In other words, although the kingdom cannot be observed, it can be realized by means of a mind which has left all concepts behind and entered the unified simplicity of its ground, in which it is as open and trusting as a child.[2]

The gift of seeing clearly is always available, always ready to open and blossom. When we let go of our search for what was never missing, the grasping mind relaxes and the kingdom begins to appear. It's as present when we're washing up or cleaning the toilet as when we are sitting silently in prayer. It can manifest at any moment, anywhere; perhaps when we want our meditation practice to be quiet and blissful and someone insists on calling for us; or when the dog just won't stop barking; or when our computer has just crashed for the tenth time in a row; or perhaps when we've been trying to scrub burnt food off the bottom of a frying pan for half an hour. Like a seed buried in the soil of our life, the kingdom is waiting for us to water and tend to it. It is part and parcel of who we are.

---

[1] Hilarion Alfeyev, *The Spiritual World of Isaac the Syrian* (Kalamazoo, MI: Cistercian Publications, 2000), p. 267.

[2] To explore this further, look at Chapter 4 of the fourteenth-century work *The Cloud of Unknowing*.

25

THE FRUIT OF SELF-FORGETFULNESS

'Gardening can be understood as a form of space-time medicine', says Dr Sue Stuart-Smith, author of the highly acclaimed book *The Well-Gardened Mind: The Restorative Power of Nature*. In an interview for a *New York Times* article,[1] Stuart Smith, a practising psychiatrist, describes gardening as 'an accessible form of creativity [which] allows us to bring something new into the world.' What Stuart-Smith says about gardening as a therapeutic activity, and the peace to be discovered in self-forgetfulness, resonates deeply with the wisdom and healing processes of meditation. Gardeners come to see and accept their participation in a creative process much larger than themselves, which holds everything, in which you can 'lose' yourself and 'find' yourself, and touch a place of calm and peace.

> There is a paradox here: Gardening is empowering, and it's also disempowering. It feels enormously empowering to harvest your own pumpkins and share your delicious tomatoes. You know you've made something good happen, and you can share the pleasure and the nourishment. I see gardening as a coming together of human creative energy and nature's creative energy. This can make it more accessible than other creative, therapeutic activities. Learning to paint, you start with a blank canvas – it's all down to you. In the garden, we are facilitating a creative process, and we can feel

---

[1] Sue Stuart-Smith, 'Why Gardening Offers a "Psychological Lifeline" in Times of Crisis', *New York Times*, 16 March 2022, https://www.nytimes.com/2022/03/16/realestate/gardening-pyschology.html, accessed 19.03.2025.

a wonderful sense of achievement when it goes well, although really nature has done most of it. As part of that, we have to accept that we're not fully in control ...

People tend to see gardening as a hobby, an activity, but I think it's primarily a relationship. Many gardeners speak of the importance of feeling part of something larger than themselves. This is where the deeper existential experiences in the garden come from, this feeling of being part of the web of life. To be a gardener, you need to tune in to how the plants are doing, and attend to what they need. Many gardeners also testify to a feeling of receiving something in return – of being gifted, almost, whether through beauty or the food they harvest. People often describe losing themselves in the garden. Therapeutically, this is important. When the ego falls away and we are at one with a task, we experience a sense of inner calm. For people who are depressed or struggling with anxious or negative thoughts, that switching off the dialogue in their head can be very, very helpful. The immersive quality of gardening helps pull us into the present moment.

As with gardening, 'the immersive quality' of meditation gently releases us from the constricting bonds of our self-preoccupation, and helps bring us home to the gift of our life in the present moment. Just as gardeners lose themselves in the garden through a therapeutic falling-away of the ego and come to 'experience a sense of inner calm', meditators lose themselves in their practice and in self-forgetfulness touch the ever-present peace within. Remember the message at the heart of the Christian contemplative tradition: the peace we seek (all we ultimately seek) is right here, buried in the soil of our life like a precious jewel, even as our life might be feeling very far from peaceful. God is our being,[2] and therefore closer to us than we are to ourselves,[3] and so we need not worry ourselves by thinking we need to find what isn't missing. Rather, we need to

---

[2] *The Book of Privy Counselling*, Chapter 1, in *The Cloud of Unknowing and Other Works*, trans. A. C. Spearing (London: Penguin Books, 2001), p. 104.

[3] St Augustine, *Confessions*, trans. Henry Chadwick (Oxford: Oxford University Press, 1998), III, iv (11), p. 43.

realize what is always present and always available, because it is the very essence of who we are. This realization is not something we can bring about. It is all gift. Our only work is the slow, steady business of allowing ourselves to receive this gift.

Gardening, says Stuart-Smith, is primarily a relationship. So, too, is the practice of meditation (and all prayer). Both the gardener and the meditator have to accept that they're 'not fully in control'. Both lose themselves and find themselves by way of engaged, receptive release. This releasing, in which we lose ourselves and find ourselves, has nothing at all to do with achieving special mental states or special feelings, with what we do or don't experience during meditation. We cannot lose ourselves as long as we continue to grip tightly to the idea of someone trying to get hold of something, or experience something. It's difficult to become self-forgetful if we are always remembering ourselves. Instead, like quiet gardeners, we learn to be content with gently tilling the soil of the present moment. We learn to work with whatever happens to be here, and trust that God has everything in hand.

The wisdom and healing processes of meditation unfold out of sight, like germinating seeds. But the fruits of our practice shine in the quality of our relationships, in our care of each other and of the world; they shine as the radiance of our essential being, which is love (Matt. 7.20; 1 John 4.7–8).

26

THE EXPERIENCE OF ONENESS

When Jesus was asked which is the first among all the commandments, he answered that the first is to hear (to know) that God is *one* and to love this *one* with our whole being. Then he joined a second commandment to the first — that we must love our neighbour as ourself, saying there is no other commandment greater than these (Mark 12.28–34). *Knowing* the oneness of being cannot be separated from *manifesting* this oneness. To paraphrase St Augustine, all those who see and love the light of oneness are one.[1] All talk of separateness is radically qualified in its loving light.

The path of meditation leads us beyond our words and doctrines to the depths of our being. The simple practice loosens the glue of conditioning and habit that keeps our attention stuck to whatever is happening in the *foreground* of our life, so that the *background*, the oneness which is the source and context of our life, becomes increasingly apparent.

The ancient metaphor of a wheel can help us in thinking about this journey. Imagine an old-fashioned cartwheel and that you are one of the spokes. Our journey begins where the spoke meets the outer rim of the wheel, at what appears to be the farthest point away from the hub. When you look sideways from this point, you appear to be separate from all the other spokes, at a distance from them. Now, imagine you're travelling down your spoke towards the centre of the wheel. This is the journey of meditation. Day by day

---

[1] St Augustine, *Confessions*, trans. Henry Chadwick (Oxford: Oxford University Press, 1998), Book 10.

you faithfully meditate, content to simply say your prayer word and follow your breath, trusting that this is enough, diligently letting go of every thought, especially any thoughts about progress. As the weeks and months go past, it seems that the other spokes are getting closer. That's good. In fact, it's rather wonderful. But you let go of that thought too and carry on.

Then you come to the hub. And you see that you and all the other spokes are rooted in and radiate out from this one centre, and that you are also all connected to the rim, and so are not really separate at all. From the perspective of the Centre – from what you might call God's perspective – *nothing* has changed, everything is just as it has always been. But from our perspective, *everything* seems to have changed.

The closer we come to the Centre, the closer we come to each other and to all creation. Until the illusion of separateness is overcome. Arriving at our common home, we realize that we never left, but simply forgot.

27

WHEN LIFE BECOMES PRAYER AND PRAYER BECOMES LIFE

'Be peaceful within yourself,' says St Isaac the Syrian, 'and heaven and earth will be at peace with you. Be diligent to enter into the treasury that is within you, and so you will see the treasury of Heaven: for these are one and the same, and with one entry you will behold them both. The ladder of the Kingdom is within you, hidden within your mind.'[1] We come to know God through coming to know ourselves. All that obscures this knowledge is our preoccupation with the activity of the discursive mind. As we learn to greet this activity with ever greater silence, we come to be at peace within ourselves and enter into the 'treasury' of awareness.

It's very traditional in Christianity to speak of three degrees or levels of prayer.[2] We begin with prayer of the lips, oral prayer. Next comes prayer of the mind. You will recognize this more inward way of prayer in our simple practice of meditation. 'Contain your mind within the words of prayer', says St John Climacus. The repetition of a prayer word in tandem with the flow of our breath, combined with the energy of attention, helps bring body and mind into ever greater harmony. The final level of prayer is traditionally spoken of as 'prayer of the heart' or 'prayer of the mind in the heart', and

---

[1] St Isaac the Syrian, *Ascetical Homilies* 2, trans. Holy Transfiguration Monastery, revised 2nd edition (Boston, MA: Holy Transfiguration Monastery, 2020), p. 121 (translation altered slightly).

[2] Though we must remember that all progression in the spiritual life is essentially unchartable and beyond our sight, and we should be careful not to become preoccupied with our spiritual progress.

is entirely a matter of grace. By 'heart' is meant our deep centre, the ground of our being where God ceaselessly flows into us as the Life of our life, our 'deepest me'. At this level of prayer, the thinking mind becomes so still that it forgets itself. When this happens, we are not consciously engaged in any activity called prayer. Forgetting itself, the mind relaxes, opens and falls away. Prayer of the mind has blossomed into a spacious openness to life, a way of being. We have *become* prayer.

Just as a wave arises from and appears on the ocean, so the thinking mind arises from and appears within the ocean of awareness. Just as a wave relaxes back into the ocean from which it arose, the thinking mind that has been brought to stillness relaxes back into the ocean of awareness from which it arose. Temporarily relieved of its activity, the mind comes back to the heart-of-mind, to awareness. Prayer and life, life and prayer melt into one act, one harmonious flow. 'When the intellect is no longer dissipated among external things or dispersed across the world through the senses,' writes St Basil, 'it returns to itself; and by means of itself it ascends to the thought [knowledge] of God.'³ Our meditation, our prayer, stops being 'ours'. We are taken into the silent life of God, the Life of all life.

Most if not all of us will have experienced moments when our thinking mind relaxed and fell away. There is nothing magic or esoteric about this. We are designed for it. It might have been when we looked into the eyes of someone we adore. It might have happened when we were lost in a piece of music – or in the moment of silence after the final note. Perhaps it happened when we were weeding the garden or lying in a warm bath after a tiring day. This falling away of the mind in daily life (which happens more frequently than we might imagine) goes largely unnoticed and unrecognized. It is simply enjoyed. If we do notice, it is often recognized as the experience of peace, of connectedness and wholeness.

'At the centre of our being', writes Thomas Merton,

---

³ St Basil the Great, Letter 2, trans. Deferrari, pp. 12–14, quoted in Bishop Kallistos Ware, *The Orthodox Way* (Yonkers, NY: St Vladimir's Press, 1995), p. 61.

is a point ... of pure truth, a point or spark which belongs entirely to God ... which is inaccessible to the fantasies of our own mind or the brutalities of our own will. This little point ... is the pure glory of God in us. It is so to speak his name written in us ... It is like a pure diamond, blazing with the invisible light of heaven. It is in everybody, and if we could see it, we would see these billions of points of light coming together in the face and blaze of a sun that would make all the darkness and cruelty of life vanish completely ... The gate of heaven is everywhere.[4]

As we have heard Clement of Alexandria say, 'The most beautiful and the greatest learning is to know oneself; for whoever knows their self knows God; and if they know God, they will become like Him.'[5]

---

[4] Thomas Merton, *Conjectures of a Guilty Bystander* (New York: Image Books, Doubleday, 1968), p. 158.

[5] Clement of Alexandria, *The Pedagogue* III, 1 (1,1), quoted in *The Kiss: The Beshara Talks of Dom Sylvester Houédard* (Cheltenham: Beshara Publications, 2022), p. 205 (translation altered slightly).

28

IN YOUR LIGHT WE SEE LIGHT

When we begin our journey of meditation (and we are, in a sense, always beginning), it's a little like setting off to walk slowly up a mountain. At the foot of the mountain we cannot see very far. The horizon is obscured by the bushes and trees that surround us. Holding our thoughts and the content of our moment-to-moment experience close, it's difficult to see beyond them. Grasping the sense of self that is derived from the constant activity of the mind, we are convinced there is someone here who can't see very far.

After a little deliberation, we set off on the path up the mountain. And after walking for a couple of hours, we decide it's time to sit down and have a short rest. Lifting our water bottle to our lips, we notice how far we've come already. The bushes and trees that clustered close around us at the foot of the mountain now look small and distant, almost like toys. Looking out over the opening countryside, something within us starts to relax. We begin to sense how small we are, and we don't mind at all. Slowly, steadily, we push on, keeping our eyes on the path before us. Concentrating a little more now on putting one foot in front of the other, our breaths and steps fall into a quiet harmony. An hour or so later (much to our happy relief), we finally reach the top. And looking out towards the distant horizon something wonderful happens. Suddenly beholding the vastness and the beauty before us, we forget ourselves, disappearing in this moment of quiet awe. All that is left is wholeness, connectedness, as if all the moving pieces of our life have silently fallen into place. We *disappear* and discover ourselves extraordinarily *here*.

After some time – how much exactly, we can't say, though the cooler air hints at the passing hours – we begin our descent. After an hour or so, we stop to rest at the halfway point. From the rucksack, we retrieve a volume of St Augustine's homilies on the Gospel of John. Opening it, our eyes settle on the words: 'He must increase, I must decrease' (John 3.30, NRSVUK). The words echo and resonate deeply in us. The sense of what we encountered at the top of the mountain flows quietly through us again. Everything seems to have changed. Yet everything is just as it was. We have glimpsed what Evagrius spoke of as open country whose name is prayer.[1]

'He must increase, I must decrease ...' The more we know God, says St Augustine, 'the more we understand, the more it seems as if God grows in us, but God does not *grow* or *change* in any way.'[2] What grows is our understanding. What appears as the growth of God within us is actually *our* growth, *our* opening within God, as we become increasingly present to God's ever-present presence. As all that obstructs the eye of awareness is gently washed away, our spiritual sight is restored. We begin to see light; a little at first, then a little more, and then yet more. It seems at first that the light is growing within us. But the light is complete. It doesn't grow or change in any way. 'It is like that too with your inner self,' says Augustine, 'you make progress in God, and God seems to grow in you; yet in fact you are diminishing.'[3] Augustine is not saying that who we *really* are diminishes, but that our *ideas* of who we are diminish in the light of awareness. 'In your light, we see light', sang the psalmist (Ps. 36.9, NRSVUK). In your light we see who we are, that we are light from light.

Whatever happens in our life, whatever suffering befalls us, whatever suffering we might have caused others, as St Teresa of Avila reminds and encourages us, 'The fountainhead that shines like the sun from the centre of the soul never loses its radiance. It is ever-present within the soul and nothing can diminish its beauty.'[4]

---

[1] See Chapter 61 in *The Praktikos and Chapters on Prayer by Evagrius Ponticus* (Cistercian Publications, 1981), p. 65.

[2] *The Works of St Augustine, A Translation for the 21st Century, Homily 14, Homilies on the Gospel of John*, 1–40, trans. Edmund Hill OP (New York: New City Press, 2009), pp. 264–5 (emphasis added).

[3] *The Works of St Augustine*, pp. 264–5.

[4] St Teresa of Avila, *The Interior Castle*, trans. Miribai Starr (New York: Riverhead Books, 2003), p. 42.

29

'*EPHPHATHA!*' BE OPENED!

When we reflect on living fully, living well, most of us will recognize the moments when our fears and attachments have closed us off from the natural openness of our heart. How might we have met situations we found challenging with more peace and compassion? How might we have greeted the changing circumstances of life with more openness, without trying to grasp and control?

One Saturday afternoon when I was eight or nine years old, I can remember being taken to the cinema to see a popular children's film. I can't remember anything at all about the film we went to see, but I was very struck by something in the short educational documentary they showed before it. Scientists studying a type of monkey put some nuts in a hollow log, then retreated to watch what happened. One of the monkeys, who'd been observing all this closely from a nearby tree, came down to explore. Spotting the nuts through a hole halfway down the log, it reached inside and grabbed a handful. A few seconds later, the scientists slowly approached. The monkey was alarmed. It called out loudly and tried to pull its hand out of the log so it could get away. But it wouldn't let go of the nuts. And as long as it continued to grasp hold of them, its closed hand wouldn't fit through the hole.

Learning to meet our life with more openness and less grasping is a central theme in meditation. It is a skill and an orientation which helps open us to the preciousness of life and lessens our suffering as we navigate its flow. The grasping mind wants everything nailed down on its own terms. It struggles against the openness needed to flow with life's flow. Recognizing this tendency in ourselves, we can learn to open the closed hand of the mind and greet life with our open heart.

When it's needed, being able to apply the gift of narrow, focused attention is hugely valuable. It helped the monkey find the nuts. It helped our ancestors find food without becoming the food of something else. Without this gift we would find it all but impossible to carry out our daily life. But this gift needs to be balanced with an even greater gift: the open awareness of the heart. It helps us see how our current concerns and preoccupations fit into the wider flow and meaning of our life. Knowing how and when to release our grip on what might need releasing, we are released. Without the gift of open awareness, we can quickly become fearful of the unavoidable disappointments and losses that come with the natural precariousness and the insecurity of our existence. Our inner resistance to this can all too easily veil the open awareness of our heart and close us off from those around us. Seeing and relaxing the grasping mind, we are brought back into relationship. Speaking of our relationship with God, Martin Laird writes: 'We become ever more present to [God's] Presence only by way of release and receptivity. Not through the calculating grasp of acquisition.'[1] So too in our relationships with each other. We become present to the presence of others by way of release and receptivity. We come into relationship through opening.

In the Gospel of Mark, we find Jesus using a small but deeply significant word as he brings healing, a word which has been said to sum up the whole of Christ's message and all his work (Mark 7.31–37). Recorded in the language Jesus spoke to draw our attention to it, the word is *'Ephphatha'*, which means 'Be opened'. When Jesus was travelling across an area known as the Decapolis, a man was brought to him for healing who couldn't hear and had difficulty speaking. Jesus takes the man off by himself away from the crowd. In this quieter place Jesus touches the man's ears and tongue, looks up to heaven, and with a deep sigh says: *'Ephphatha!'* ('Be opened!'). And immediately the man begins to hear and to speak plainly.

---

[1] Martin Laird, *An Ocean of Light: Contemplation, Transformation, and Liberation* (Oxford: Oxford University Press, 2019), p. 27.

Notice where the healing takes place. Jesus takes the man away from the crowd to a quieter place where he can be alone with him. Meister Eckhart says that in order to realize our oneness with God, we have to come away from 'the crowd' of our thoughts and feelings and moment-to-moment experience. For awareness of oneness to open and 'shine forth truly and clearly' we must let go all that is brought in from *without* through the senses, and open ourselves to what is always welling up from *within*.[2] Away from the crowd, in the quieter place, Jesus touches the man and says, '*Ephphatha!*' ('Be opened!').

One effect of the healing is that the man can now hear and speak. All that had made it difficult to communicate and contributed to his isolation from community is 'opened'. The healing is an opening to those around him and to the world. But '*Ephphatha*' is also an invitation to be opened to the deepest truth of who we are, to hear that we are not separate from each other, but one in the oneness of God. We can say that this little word sums up the whole of Christ's message and all his work because he came to 'open' us into the fullness of relationship.

Each time we meditate, we come away with Christ to a quieter place, to listen to the Word that is ceaselessly spoken in our heart, that we might *hear* the voice of Love, that we might *become* the voice of Love.

---

[2] *The Complete Mystical Works of Meister Eckhart, Sermon 4*, trans. Maurice O'C. Walshe (New York: The Crossroad Publishing Company, 2009), pp. 55–61.

30

A NEW RELATIONSHIP WITH TIME

'Time is what we want most, but what, alas! we use worst', observed the influential Quaker William Penn (1644–1718). Many of us have a difficult relationship with time. We might wish we had more of it to finish that home project which never quite gets done. We might wish we were more efficient at using the time we do have, having chased our tail all day, before we fall into bed. We might regret the time we have spent on certain things in the past, or worry about what is likely to consume our time in the future. It's all too easy to feel we are the victim of time. 'In our culture,' notes the writer and lay Benedictine Kathleen Norris, 'time can seem like an enemy: it chews us up and spits us out with appalling ease.'[1]

Like Norris, I was raised with little or no idea of monasticism as a living wisdom tradition; and it wasn't until I went to live with the Benedictines of Prinknash Abbey and participated in the daily rhythm of the Liturgy of the Hours (the Divine Office) that my relationship with time began to change. I was unexpectedly reminded of this a few years ago. Not by a bell ringing out from a Cotswold hillside, but by the beautiful undulating call to prayer filling the air of Istanbul with an invitation to acknowledge the Divine. Five times a day we were invited to pause our activity and participate in a rhythm of remembrance which Benedictines speak of as 'the sanctification of time'.

'The monastic perspective', says Norris, 'welcomes time as a gift from God, and seeks to put it to good use rather than allowing us

---

[1] Kathleen Norris, *The Cloister Walk* (New York: Riverhead Books, 1997), p. xix.

to be used up by it.' Norris continues, 'A friend who was educated by the Benedictines has told me that she owes to them her sanity with regard to time. "You never really finish anything in life," she says, "and while that's humbling, and frustrating, it's all right. The Benedictines, more than any other people I know, insist that there is time in each day for prayer, for work, for study, and for play."'[2] Liturgical time is essentially poetic time, oriented towards process rather than productivity, willing to wait attentively in stillness rather than always pushing to 'get the job done'.

I'm fortunate to have the privilege of listening to people talk about their journey on the path of meditation. In a culture which so often presents time as a relentless taskmaster, it's wonderful to hear from so many how daily meditation has helped bring about a radically new perspective on so many aspects of their life, including time. The time we give to meditation (like liturgical time) is essentially 'poetic time'. Instead of trying to produce something, we participate within its gentle wisdom and healing process. Rather than trying to achieve anything, we learn to greet each moment with simple, open attentiveness.

'Good liturgy', writes Maggie Ross,

> provides a context in which our subtle senses, dulled by daily toil, can reawaken. It is not the liturgy that sanctifies our lives; our lives are already sacred, and liturgy tries to remind us of that. The hours of the Divine Office do not sanctify the day; they bring us to remembrance that the day is already holy and we have the privilege of living it.[3]

So, too, with meditation. The simple practice provides a sanctuary in which we can release all that needs releasing and allow our subtle senses to reawaken. We learn to receive each day, each moment, as a gift from God that we can use well, rather than allowing ourselves to be swept along and used up by it. Saying our prayer word,

---

[2] Norris, *The Cloister Walk*, p. xix.

[3] Maggie Ross, *Writing the Icon of the Heart – In Silence Beholding* (Eugene, OR: Cascade Books, 2013), from the chapter 'Liturgy in Truth'.

following our breath, we are brought to remembrance that our life is already sacred, that the day is already holy, and we have the privilege of living it.

Eternity is our home, even in the midst of time. We already dwell in the silent eternity of God's love by virtue of God's love indwelling us. It is only our noisy thoughts and distractedness that pull us away from this. From a cultural point of view, we inhabit a world which is sustained by distractedness, which is out of harmony and out of balance. Our minds are crowded with unimportant information. The frantic speed required to simply hold our ground in our artificial world causes enormous anxiety. 'I have often said that the sole cause of man's unhappiness is that he does not know how to stay quietly in his room', wrote Blaise Pascal. But it doesn't have to be this way. In the face of our relentless consumer culture, we have the freedom to make a deeply subversive decision, to see and act in a radically counter-cultural way. The opportunity to centre ourselves in silence instead of noise, to act with care instead of carelessness, is before us every moment. We can choose harmony and balance. We can live and love from the wellspring of divine silence and make the most of the precious gift of time.

31

TRAVELLING LIGHTLY – LIVING FULLY

In her wonderful book, *Upon This Mountain: Prayer in the Carmelite Tradition*, Sister Mary McCormack OCD speaks about her experience of following a way of prayer that is about stillness of mind, surrender and release. 'During long years of struggle and darkness,' writes Sister Mary,

> I finally learned to let go of everything else. In that time ... every idea of the God to whom I would direct my prayer just withered away, [such] that, in the time of prayer, I could only be. In the end, there was not even the slightest flicker of anything that you or I would identify as prayer ... I even stopped protesting. Very, very slowly (and words fail me here), I became aware that there was now absolutely nothing between my raw reality and the utter reality of God. I understood that any concept of God veiled him more than it conveyed him, and that my reaching out to God was only distracting me from the immediacy of his presence.[1]

In meditation, we set out on a journey like no other. Saying our prayer word, following our breath, we learn to travel lightly. Instead of packing, we unpack. Instead of trying to grasp hold of what cannot be grasped, we allow ourselves to be held. Instead of worrying about finding God, or experiencing God, we allow ourselves

---

[1] Mary McCormack OCD, *Upon This Mountain: Prayer in the Carmelite Tradition* (Oxford: Teresian Press, 2009), Chapter 3, 'Into Stillness'.

to rest in God's presence. We learn how our concepts veil what cannot be conceived, how our images of God cause us to overlook the One who cannot be imagined. We accept Jesus' invitation to the rich young man to divest himself of all his valued possessions (Matt. 19.21) and follow our teacher's path of total self-emptying (Phil. 2.1–6). Saying our prayer word, following our breath, we look beyond what our mind and senses can grasp. We learn to surrender everything, that we might come home to the truth of everything. The gateway to the kingdom, Jesus tells us, involves a total self-emptying, a releasing which opens us to receive more than we could ever ask for. It is only our hesitations, our second thoughts, our lack of trust, that cause us to overlook the gift which shines in each of us and which we are created to enjoy. 'Take nothing for the journey', Jesus told his Disciples (Mark 6.8).

'The Kingdom of Heaven', says Evagrius, 'is apatheia [inner peace] of the soul [mind] along with true knowledge of existing things.'[2] St John Cassian, the famous student of Evagrius who was largely responsible for bringing this way of meditation to the West, translated apatheia as 'purity of heart' (*puritas cordis*), the bliss, beatitude or reward of which is that the pure of heart shall enjoy the gift of the contemplation of God (Matt. 5.8).[3] With this in mind, remember how St Isaac the Syrian spoke of the kingdom as the gift of contemplation, of transfigured awareness. From the earliest centuries of Christianity, a great cloud of witnesses have spoken of the kingdom as a *present* reality, something internal, not external, which becomes manifest as God helps us to establish peace within ourselves; that the foundation for a wholly different future is to be found in the very heart of who we are. The possibility of a more just and loving world is not an idea or a concept, but a reality to be seen, touched and made visible in our relationships (1 John 1.1–3). We are invited to know the infinite love of Christ that exceeds all knowing (Eph. 3.19), to *live* this love, to become places where the kingdom *happens*.

---

[2] Evagrius Ponticus, *The Praktikos and Chapters on Prayer*, Cistercian Studies Series 4 (Kalamazoo, MI: Cistercian Publications, 1981), p. 15.

[3] See the *Conferences* of St John Cassian, particularly Conferences 9 and 10 on prayer.

Over time, writes Sister Mary,

> I came to recognize that moments of such formless prayer had a substance that deeply satisfied and sustained me. I also became aware of an effect in my response to life ... Inner rules that had always governed me began to give way to something more free and authentic. As I learned to tolerate 'unknowing' in prayer, I became more at ease with the questions and perplexities of human existence in our uncertain age. I became conscious of a simple oneness with God that pervaded everything in life, without effort on my part, and there was also the beginning of a sense of oneness with the rest of humanity and with all of creation.[4]

---

[4] McCormack, *Upon This Mountain*, Chapter 3, 'Into Stillness'.

32

SEEING CREATION AS RADIANCE

Since the earliest centuries, Christians have spoken of the visible, material world as pointing to an invisible, immaterial source and harmony in God. St Paul saw creation as the radiance, the revelation, of the Divine. In his Letter to the Romans, he writes, 'Ever since the creation of the world, his invisible attributes of eternal power and divinity have been able to be understood and perceived in what he has made' (Rom. 1.20, NAB). Although Paul quickly goes on to say that people *didn't* see this, that they were unable to read the book of creation, which St Augustine called the first Bible. St Gregory of Nyssa, writing in the fourth century, says that the partially developed mind believes that the beautiful things it encounters are beautiful in their own nature, but that 'someone who has purified the eyes of their mind, and is trained to see beautiful things ... makes use of the visible as a springboard to rise to contemplation of the spiritual.'[1] St Ephrem the Syrian, also writing in the fourth century, sings of how all things (and each of us) are symbols, expressions of the indwelling presence of the Divine. 'Lord, your symbols are everywhere ... yet You are hidden from everywhere. Blessed is the Hidden One shining out!'[2]

It's not surprising that people find it so difficult to see creation (and themselves) as the radiance of the Divine. Our culture encourages us to strongly affirm what presents itself to us through our senses, the content of experience, what appears to us as material

---

[1] Gregory of Nyssa, *On Virginity*, quoted in *The Roots of Christian Mysticism* by Olivier Clément (New York: New City Press, 1982), p. 218 (translation altered slightly).

[2] Sebastian Brock, *The Luminous Eye: The Spiritual World Vision of Saint Ephrem* (Piffard, NY: Cistercian Publications, 1992), p. 55.

reality. We are, in a sense, trained to overlook the infinite reality which is ceaselessly disclosing itself to us in and *through* the material, the immaterial source in which 'all things were created' (Col. 1.16, NAB), 'in which we live and move and have our being' (Acts 17.28, NRSVUK). Unable to see creation as divine radiance, it's all too easy for us to value things in and of themselves, and to conceive of creation as separate from God and from ourselves. The great and all too evident danger of the illusion of separateness is that this false *conceptual* distance can quickly become an *emotional* distance, and then a *moral* distance. Meditation helps us come to see created reality for what it truly is, something we are inextricably part of and bound up with, rather than something wholly external to us, which we might simply use or dominate.

In his *Confessions*, St Augustine writes of a grace-filled moment he shared with his beloved mother Monica shortly before she died.[3] His luminous words speak of the life-changing work of silence and the gift of contemplation, the gift of *seeing clearly*.

> We were on our own, talking,
> and our conversation was easy and happy.
> Putting aside thoughts of the past,
> we gazed into the future,
> looking at it in the light of Truth,
> which means in your light.
> And we asked ourselves what the life of your saints
> would be like, that life which 'no eye has seen,
> nor ear heard, nor heart has conceived'.
>
> We placed the mouths of our hearts
> at the stream of divine water
> that flows from the fountain of life,
> which is you …
>
> We came to our own souls,
> and passed beyond them …

---

[3] *Confessions*, Book 9, trans. Benignus O'Rourke (London: Darton, Longman and Todd, 2013).

While we spoke of eternal Wisdom and breathed it in,
we for an instant, and with a great leap of our heart,
reached out and touched it.
We sighed, and leaving there the first fruits of our spirit,
we returned to the sound of our own voices,
and to words which have a beginning and an end ...

Then we said:
'If the tumult within us could be silent.
If the thoughts and images of earth,
of water and of air,
and of the heavens,
were to be silent;
and even if our very soul
became so silent
that we no longer thought of ourselves
so that we might pass beyond self.
If dreams and all the fantasies
of our imagination were silent,
and if every tongue
and every noise
were hushed;
and all things
that are merely passing
in this world
grew silent.

For all these, could we but listen,
would say to us,
'We did not make ourselves.
The One who made us abides for ever.'

It's wonderful to know that God shines within us and all creation. But the deepest wisdom is that God shines *as* us, that creation is – we all are – *theophany*, 'God appearing.'

Part Four

PEACE IN THE WORLD

*Who you are is more
beautiful than you imagine.
For that you is God.*

33

EMPTYING OURSELVES OF SELF

Behind a temple there was a field where there were many squashes growing on a vine. One day a fight broke out among them, with the squashes in two groups, shouting at one another. The head priest heard the uproar and, stepping outside to see what was going on, found the squashes quarrelling. The priest scolded them. 'What are you doing out there fighting? You should meditate, not fight!'

While the squashes were sitting in meditation, their anger subsided and they settled down. Then the priest said quietly, 'Everyone put your hand on top of your head.' When the squashes felt the top of their heads, they found some strange thing attached there. It turned out to be the vine that connected them all together.

'This is really strange,' they said. 'Here we've been arguing when actually we're all tied together and living just one life.'[1]

One of the greatest gifts of meditation is how it helps heal us of the illusion of separateness, the misperception that veils our essential interconnectedness. As we've noted before, the great and all too evident danger of this illusion is that it deeply influences how we relate to each other and the world. A false conceptual distance can quickly become an emotional distance and a moral distance.

How does the illusion of separateness arise? It arises in large part

---

[1] Adapted from the tale as set out in Kosho Uchiyama, *Opening the Hand of Thought*, trans. and ed. Tom Wright, Jisho Warner and Shohaku Okumura (Somerville, MA: Wisdom Publications, 2004), pp. 77–8.

from the noisy chatter of the thinking (discursive) mind, which likes to categorize and parcel up the world of our experience into tidy separate boxes, giving rise to a strong sense of 'I' and 'you', of 'mine' and 'yours'. In meditation we follow a path of self-forgetfulness which unfolds quite naturally as we focus our attention on something other than ourselves. The simple practice progressively brings the thinking mind to greater and greater stillness and silence. And as this happens, our sense of separateness starts to dissolve. What we might previously have taken to be solid dividing lines between us and God, and between each other, become porous before the quiet light of awareness. Notions of distinguishing identity we may have held for many years become increasingly transparent before this loving light, until they eventually evaporate within it.

The illusion of separateness causes us to imagine we are in some way separate from the vine which gives us life and apart from which we could not exist (John 15.1–17). Emptying ourselves of self, we discover the infinite fullness of our shared life in God (see Phil. 2.5–7). The old Japanese tale about the angry squashes speaks delightfully simply about the problem and the antidote to be found in stillness and silence. When the squashes became still and quiet – when they let go of their angry thoughts – they discovered they were not separate at all, but intimately connected. Their new way of seeing opened into a new way of being. To those that know they are one with the vine, all talk of difference and separateness becomes unimportant. From time to time people ask me, 'If I let go of all my thoughts, all my ideas about who I am and how the world is, what is going to be left of me?' The only answer I can give is, 'What will be left of you is *you*. What will be left is a ray of God's light.'

We meditate to know we are one with the vine. How does this oneness register in our awareness? It is 'like rain falling from the sky onto a river or pool', says St Teresa of Avila. 'There is nothing but water. It's impossible to divide the sky water from the land water. When a little stream enters the sea, who could separate out its waters again?'[2] The realization of oneness is the deepest foundation of peace

---

[2] St Teresa of Avila, *The Interior Castle*, trans. Miribai Starr (New York: Riverhead Books, 2003), p. 270.

within us, and the foundation of peace between us. It is the deepest basis for compassion and justice, for our care of each other and of our precious world. To discover that we are one with the vine is to discover that everyone and everything is one within the oneness of the vine. 'When it is truly seen,' wrote Julian of Norwich, 'no person can separate themselves from another.'[3]

---

[3] Julian of Norwich, *The Revelations of Divine Love*, trans. Barry Windeatt (Oxford: Oxford University Press, 2015), p. 138.

34

AT-ONE-MENT

The illusion of separateness is a great affliction for so many today. The feeling of loneliness, of alienation, of not being able to deeply connect with others, is a cause of so much suffering. But it doesn't have to be this way. The prerequisite for knowing the oneness of being is to be at one, in harmony, with ourselves. This is the heart of the meaning of atonement. Through grace, our at-one-ment with ourselves opens into at-one-ment with each other, and with the whole of creation in the oneness of God.

We do not come to this by a process of thought or analysis, through grasping subtle theological or metaphysical propositions, but through stillness of mind, through clearing a space in which to encounter the essential oneness of our being. The invitation of meditation is to let go of our thoughts (including those that might appear intensely interesting and wonderfully holy), and to come home to the simple suchness of life, unmediated by our stories about it. For some people hearing about meditation for the first time, it can come as a surprise to hear that letting go of thoughts includes letting go of thoughts about God during our time of practice. It becomes much more understandable if people liken meditation to being with someone they love to be with. Our whole understanding of prayer becomes much simpler. When we are with someone we love to be with, we can rest from thinking about them. We can simply enjoy being with them. We are both right here. And likewise with God, who doesn't know how to be absent or anywhere else but right here. When we let go of our thoughts *about* someone we are with, we are simply with them. When we let go of our thoughts *about* God, all that remains is God's unmediated presence.

35

RESTING IN AWARENESS

'Come away by yourselves to a solitary place and rest awhile,' Jesus encourages us (Mark 6.31). 'Come to me, all you who toil and are burdened, and I will give you rest' (Matt. 11.28).

The anonymous medieval author of *The Book of Privy Counselling* (who also wrote *The Cloud of Unknowing*) gives a wonderful teaching about the simplicity of meditation. As someone from our practice community put it, 'The simplicity of the practice means that anyone can do it. And anything that is really going to change the world has to be accessible to everyone.' It is enough, the author teaches, to rest in simple awareness of our being. In this simple awareness we are 'oned' with God, with peace itself, to *become* that peace.

> It is not beyond anyone to learn this simple practice. It is so simple that I quietly marvel and smile to myself when I hear highly educated people say that this teaching is so difficult, so profound, so subtle, that it can hardly be grasped by the greatest scholar or intelligent man or woman alive. People become so blinded by their cleverness and learning that they overlook the utter simplicity of meditation and cannot understand it. Trying to grasp it with the intellect, they can no more gain an understanding of this easy practice than a young child learning their ABCs could understand the knowledge of the greatest scholar. And yet by this simple practice, even the most simple and uneducated person in the world is oned to God in loving humility and perfect love.
>
> Here is my advice. Don't focus on *what* you are, but rest in

simple awareness *that* you are. Allow yourself to descend to the deepest point of your mind, and letting go of any desire to *know* what you are, rest in simple awareness *that* you are.

It requires all the gifts of our learning and much skilful use of your intelligence to comprehend what you are. But to rest in simple awareness that we are is something you can do without need of any special cleverness or natural gifts. And if you happen to be feeling awful about yourself and so burdened that you are unsure what to do with yourself, here is some more advice to help you: take God just as he is. Accept his good graciousness and press him against yourself as naturally as you would a plain and simple plaster or warm compress when you are sick. Lay him against yourself, just as you are.

Step up, then. Be bold and try this simple remedy: lift yourself up (just as you are) to God (just as he is) without any attempt to analyze yourself or God. And stop trying to determine whether anything is good or bad, divine or human, grace-given or from your nature. The most important thing is your simple awareness of your naked being. In this simple awareness you will be carried in willingness of love to be oned in grace and spirit in the precious being of God, just as he is – without anything more.

But be prepared for your unruly thinking mind to react. When your anxious mind can find nothing in the practice to grab hold of and chew on, it will start to complain. It will urge you to give up this work and do something (anything!) to satisfy its hungry curiosity. It will try and tell you that meditation is of no value and that, in fact, you are doing nothing at all. And that is precisely why I love it! For there is no work that I may do, none that may be done by my mind or body, that can bring me so near to God as this simple awareness and offering up of my blind being. So, although your thinking mind can find no food for itself in this simple practice, and might try to make you stop, do not give up, but be its master. Do not turn back to feed your thoughts with your attention, however persistent they are.

However subtle, however good, however beneficial our thoughts on our nature and life may be – they are a fragmentation and scattering in comparison with this simple awareness and offering of your being. They are a distraction from the perfection of oneness.

And so be still. Stay at the deepest level of your spirit, which is your being. And don't turn back for anything, however good or holy it may seem and to which your mind would lead you.[1]

In meditation, we learn to rest in the essential peace of our being, trusting that God has everything in hand.

---

[1] Translated from the Middle English edition of *The Cloud of Unknowing and The Book of Privy Counselling*, edited by Phyllis Hodgson (Oxford: Oxford University Press for the Early English Text Society, 1981), pp. 137–9.

36

SILENCE AND SOLIDARITY

Some years ago on BBC Radio 4, there was a short programme about the wonderful Civilizations Choir of Antakya, Turkey. The choir includes people of Alevi, Sunni, Catholic, Orthodox, Armenian and Jewish origin, and it performs songs and hymns in 12 different languages and dialects. Part-way through the programme, the presenter asked an Orthodox priest why he thought everyone in the choir got on so well. He began his answer, 'We all come from Abraham …' Not an altogether surprising thing to say, you might think. The religious traditions represented in the choir all speak of Abraham as their father in faith. But he added, '… and the silence before him', pointing directly to the ultimate ground of our solidarity, the silent, groundless ground of God. 'We all come from Abraham and the silence before him.'

'My heart was deafened by the din of my mind', wrote St Augustine, pointing to how internal mental noise can deafen us to the simple, unitive song of reality. The internal 'din' that Augustine refers to is not caused by our initial thoughts, which arise and depart as naturally as waves on the surface of the sea. The 'din' is caused by our reactive engagement with them, the stories we tell ourselves *about* ourselves and life. It is this which creates the impression of solid edges and boundaries around us, which sustains the conceptual gaps we erect between ourselves and God and everything. The practice of meditation offers us a simple remedy: greet thoughts with stillness and silence. When we notice our attention has latched on to a thought and we are busily chatting to ourselves about it, we let go of whatever story we were weaving and quietly return to our practice.

The anonymous fourteenth-century author of *The Cloud of Unknowing* offers much practical advice when it comes to minding the conceptual gaps we create. Encouraging us to avoid getting caught up in too much thinking about our practice, he highlights the particular danger of interpreting certain words physically (literally) instead of spiritually (literarily and metaphorically) and giving rise to false dualisms (gaps) and indicators of progress.[1] Writing with his characteristic blend of wisdom, directness and wit, the *Cloud* author advises, 'Where another [person] would tell you to gather your powers and your senses altogether within yourself and worship God there, I would not tell you to do that.' Rather, he counsels (I like to imagine a smile on his face when he wrote this), 'Take care that not in any manner will you be within yourself. And also, I do not want you to be outside of yourself, and not above yourself, nor behind yourself, and not on one side nor on the other.'

The *Cloud* author then imagines his student asking him (very understandably), 'Where then shall I be? Nowhere, according to you!' He replies, 'Now truly you speak well; for that is exactly where I would have you be. The reason is that nowhere physically is everywhere spiritually.' If you are caught up in too much self-conscious thinking about your practice – stop it! Be still. Be silent. Do your practice. When the conceptualizing mind is still and quiet, conceptual gaps dissolve. The illusion of distance between us evaporates.

What should we do when our physical senses tell us we are doing nothing, because they are unable to find anything in this practice to grasp and feed themselves with? 'Continue doing this nothing,' the *Cloud* author encourages,

> and do it for the love of God. Do not give up, but labour on with great effort in that nothing with a strong desire to have God whom no person can know. Don't be concerned that your senses can't sense it and you can't get your head around it. Not being able to reason about it is a sign of its infinite nature and value. Choose what the senses and thinking mind

---

[1] See *The Cloud of Unknowing*, trans. Ira Progoff (New York: Dell Publishing, 1957), Chapter 68.

will tell you is nowhere and nothing. What the 'outer' aspect of ourselves calls 'nothing', the 'inner' aspect of ourselves calls 'All' – for it teaches [us] to know the essence of things, both physical and spiritual, with no special attention to any one thing by itself [as separate].

The conceptualizing mind is an extraordinary gift, which can help bring us to the threshold of realizing our essential oneness with God and each other. But at this threshold, the threshold of wonder, it must fall silent and allow love to carry us over. God cannot be grasped by the intellect, but can be known by the heart.[2] As we learn to be still and silent, the 'gaps' between us and God and everything are revealed to be mere conventions, relative perspectives. All notions of separateness break down in the simple light of awareness.

---

[2] *The Cloud of Unknowing*, Chapter 4.

37

TOUCHING PEACE IN EVERYDAY LIFE

Alice found herself caught up in various troubles. A new senior manager at work seemed to be taking every opportunity to criticize her. One of her children was taking a year out of university due to anxiety. Her elderly parents, who wished to remain in the house that had been their home for over 50 years, were facing serious health issues and challenges with independent living. Alice's brother, who lived considerably closer to her parents, was more than happy for her to take the full weight of 'sorting things out'. So she decided to take some time off work and stay with her parents for a week to help them make plans for the future.

After dinner together on the first evening, she took a walk to clear her head. And following a path through fields and winding country lanes, lanes that she'd known and loved since childhood, she let the tears run freely. When she reached the highest point on the walk, she sat down on the grass, leant back against the trunk of a tree, and began to meditate. At first, all she was aware of was a feeling of sadness and a deep weariness. It crossed her mind to go back, but she decided to stay sitting there a little longer, that this might be the best thing she could do. Somewhere deep inside, Alice told me, she could hear the steadying rhythm of her prayer word quietly sounding, as if woven within the flow of her breath, helping to gently disentangle and release her from the churning thoughts and emotions that had followed her through the day. Looking out across the sweep of darkening fields and scattered towns to the distant horizon, she let herself touch the vastness before her. 'I suddenly felt less alone. Somehow, I knew that everyone, everything, every atom of this beautiful, delicate world, is held within a limitless field of love.'

In Chapter 5 of her Revelations, Julian of Norwich describes being shown how intimately God loves us – and the whole of creation – and where we might find peace. 'I saw that he is to us everything that is good and comforting for our help. He is our clothing that out of love enwraps us and enfolds us, embraces us and wholly encloses us, surrounding us for tender love, so that he can never leave us.'[1] Julian says she was shown a 'little thing' the size of a hazelnut lying in the palm of her hand, and looked at it trying to understand what it was, and received the answer, 'It is all that is made.' She marvels at how it could even exist, thinking it might suddenly have fallen into nothingness because of its littleness, and is answered in her understanding, 'It lasts and always will, for God loves it. And so, all things have their being by the love of God.' Julian tells us that she saw three properties in this little thing: that God made it, loves it, and keeps it, that God is 'the maker, the keeper, the lover' of all that is. She realizes that she will never have full peace and joy until she is 'oned' to God, so 'fastened' that nothing created can appear to come between them. This is the lesson of the 'little thing' that is everything, shown in the palm of Julian's hand. And we need to understand this lesson.

All created things are continually changing, arising and departing, so 'little' in this sense that were it not for God's ever-present presence as the Being of all beings, the Life of all life, everything would fall into nothingness. Knowing the nature of created things, we can know and love the uncreated ground and source of all creation. The reason we are not entirely 'in ease of heart and soul,' Julian teaches, is that we seek peace in created things, in what is 'little' and always changing. Trying to find peace in what is always *changing* causes us to overlook the *unchanging* ground and source of everything, who is true peace. God, says Julian, wishes us to know him, to rest in him, to receive the gift of spiritual peace.

Whenever we feel overwhelmed, lost, weighed down with pain, sadness or fear, we can enter the sanctuary of our practice and let

---

[1] Julian of Norwich, 'A Revelation of Love', in *The Writings of Julian of Norwich: A Vision Showed to a Devout Woman and A Revelation of Love*, ed. Nicholas Watson and Jacqueline Jenkins (University Park, PA: Pennsylvania State University Press, 2006), Chapter 5.

God show us how to meet the always-changing flow of our life more peacefully and more compassionately. It is not so much the fact that things change which causes us to suffer, but our *resistance* to this change. In meditation, we learn to meet our life, however it happens to be, with the prayer of simple, loving awareness. We come to God, to peace, 'Nakedly, plainly, and intimately.'

Alice's meditation practice helped her to find a new relationship with all that was changing, challenging and painful in her life, and touch what never changes. 'I suddenly felt less alone. Somehow, I knew that everyone, everything, every atom of this beautiful, delicate world, is held within a limitless field of love.'

38

'ME-TIME' BECOMES 'OUR-TIME'

'The role of Christians in the world', writes Elder Thaddeus, 'is to filter the atmosphere on earth and expand the atmosphere of the Kingdom of God. We can keep guard over the whole world by keeping guard over the atmosphere of heaven within us.'[1]

One of the greatest gifts that flows from meditation, from the simple prayer of stillness and silence, is how the fruit of our practice manifests as an atmosphere of peace and harmony which touches the lives of others. In his lovely book about silent prayer, *Finding Your Hidden Treasure*, Benignus O'Rourke recounts a story about the famous nineteenth-century Russian, St Seraphim of Sarov.[2] Seraphim taught that we should seek to establish peace in ourselves so that others might find peace and God *through* us.

> A young man, who had heard of Seraphim's holiness, decided to make a pilgrimage of 400 kilometres from Kiev, where he was a student, to the monastery at Sarov where Seraphim lived. The young man was very troubled in himself and he hoped that Seraphim could help him. When he arrived at the monastery, he discovered that Seraphim was now living in a hermitage an hour's walk away. So, the young man set off in the summer heat and walked through the Temniki forest until he found the little hermitage. When he arrived, there

---

[1] Ana Smiljanic, *Our Thoughts Determine Our Lives: The Life and Teachings of Elder Thaddeus Vitovnica* (Platina, CA: St Herman of Alaska Brotherhood Press, 2012), p. 66.

[2] See Benignus O'Rourke, *Finding Your Hidden Treasure* (London: Darton, Longman and Todd, 2010), Chapter 59.

was no sign of Seraphim. Walking around the little building, he eventually found the tiny figure of the monk curled up asleep at the bottom of the vegetable patch. Seraphim had been working in his garden and, taking some rest, had fallen asleep.

At first the student was very confused about what to do. He had travelled a long way to open his heart to Seraphim and seek his guidance, but didn't feel he should wake him. Then, as he stood quietly in the presence of the tiny sleeping monk, something began to happen. A deep peace began to arise within him. All that had been troubling him so deeply seemed to be evaporating. The longer he stood there, the deeper became the peace within him. Sometime later, without having exchanged a single word with Seraphim, the young man quietly left and started his journey home. The peace-filled presence of Seraphim, even asleep, had soothed the young man's suffering and brought him peace.

A small part of us might smile at the quaintness of this story, but a deeper aspect of us most likely recognizes its truth. Those of us who have experienced being in the presence of someone of deep inner peace will understand it instantly. We have all experienced the atmospheres that people radiate (peaceful or otherwise). When we find ourselves in the company of a peaceful person, we share in their peace and feel calmer in ourselves.

One time at the end of a workshop for headteachers, a person of obvious compassion and deep commitment to others said that she would love to be able to bring meditation into her life and enjoy the peace it brings. 'But', she said, 'I find it hard to allow myself *me-time*.' So I suggested she might think about meditation as the practice of *our-time*. Whatever our initial motivation to practise might be (our motivations are as varied as we are), the gift of inner peace we receive always radiates out as an atmosphere of peace which benefits others. What might initially appear to be 'me-time' (and there's nothing wrong with that) opens into 'our-time'.

Peace is a gift we cannot help sharing. Its generous, life-giving waters don't just permeate our life, but always flow outwards. If we are peaceful, we radiate peace. Even if we can't see it, we create small ripples of harmony and peace around us. As a direct, practical response to the great need for peace in our world, each of us can commit to the quiet, steady work of establishing greater peace in ourselves. This is perhaps the most important thing we can do.

39

THE GIFT OF ATTENTION

Holy people, writes Rowan Williams,

> however much they may enjoy being themselves, are not obsessively interested in themselves. They allow you to see not them, but the world around them. They allow you to see not them, but God. You come away from them feeling not, 'Oh, what a wonderful person,' but, 'What a wonderful world,' 'What a wonderful God,' or even, with surprise, 'What a wonderful person I am too.'[1]

This sort of holiness, Williams says, isn't anything to do with floating along through the ups and downs of life, being tediously saintly, barely human, probably causing people around us to feel more than a little uncomfortable. Holy people are not particularly interested in their own spiritual development. They don't think about holiness as such. They have learned to lift their attention off themselves and to give it away, to wonderful effect. The gift of attention enlarges the world, makes it a little brighter, a little warmer. People who receive the gift of attention can be helped to feel that the world is wonderful, that God is wonderful, and that they might just be wonderful too.

Ultimately, meditation, like all prayer, is not about mastering techniques, it's about *relationship*. It's not about travelling anywhere

---

[1] Rowan Williams, *Being Disciples – Essentials of the Christian Life* (London: SPCK, 2016), pp. 52–3.

or obtaining anything. Rather, it is about releasing everything that prevents us seeing, encountering, what is already here, shining within all creation. Our practice is our commitment to the quiet, steady work of simply being here, allowing God to make even the smallest aspects of our daily life more transparent to his Light.

Think of meditation as being a little like faithfully polishing a beautiful window. The point is not to *change* the window. It's fine as it is. We polish the window to let the Light pour through, into our life and through our life, to touch the lives of those around us. Not our light, but the Light that is always shining, that cannot be comprehended, but can be known in even the smallest act of kindness, compassion, friendship.

The central lesson we are learning in meditation is to pay attention, to wholly attend. When we are distracted, we are only able to give a small and distracted bit of our attention to those around us. Distractedness, living with our mind scattered in all directions, is also exhausting for us. Our practice is to lift our attention *off* ourselves and turn to the fullness of what is already here, to the fullness of relationship. As we learn to be attentive, we become better able to see and hear those around us without our own preoccupations clouding the lens of our vision, without blocking up the ear of our heart. We discover ourselves becoming more present, more available in ways we might never have expected. Quietly, almost imperceptibly, God dissolves the barriers that trap us within ourselves and isolate us from each other. We cultivate attention so we can give it away. To help people feel that the world is wonderful, that God is wonderful, that they are wonderful. To think about holiness like this can give us all great encouragement. We can all get involved in this sort of holiness.

40

THE GIFT OF PEACE

'If our thoughts are kind, peaceful and quiet,' taught Elder Thaddeus, 'turned only towards the good, then we influence ourselves and radiate peace all around us – in our family, the whole country, everywhere. When we labour in the fields of the Lord, we create harmony: divine harmony, peace and quiet spread everywhere.'[1]

Interior peace gives birth to exterior peace. If our thoughts are peaceful, we radiate peace around us, we become places of peace for our neighbour and for the world. As a direct, practical response to the circumstances in our communities that call out for greater peace, harmony and reconciliation, each of us can commit to the quiet, steady work of establishing greater peace in ourselves. This is perhaps the most important thing we can do. Everyone around us: our families, the communities we live in and work in, our entire society, will benefit from this peace. Meditation is a simple way of establishing peace that everyone can engage in.

Contemplation is very far from being a mere option for Christians, says Rowan Williams:

> it is the key to the essence of a renewed humanity that is capable of seeing the world and other subjects in the world with freedom – freedom from self-oriented, acquisitive habits and the distorted understanding that comes from them. To put it boldly, contemplation is the only ultimate answer to the

---

[1] Ana Smiljanic, *Our Thoughts Determine Our Lives: The Life and Teachings of Elder Thaddeus Vitovnica* (Platina, CA: St Herman of Alaska Brotherhood Press, 2012), p. 63.

unreal and insane world that our financial systems and our advertising culture and our chaotic and unexamined emotions encourage us to inhabit. To learn contemplative practice is to learn what we need so as to live truthfully and honestly and lovingly. It is a deeply revolutionary matter.[2]

If we can establish and protect the peace of the kingdom within us, says Elder Thaddeus,

> People will be attracted by the peace and warmth in us; they will want to be near us, and the atmosphere of heaven will gradually pass on to them. It is not even necessary to speak to people about this. The atmosphere of heaven will radiate from us even when we keep silence or talk about ordinary things. It will radiate from us even though we may not be aware of it [3]

We are called to be places of peace.
Words are optional.

---

[2] Rowan Williams, 'Archbishop Rowan Williams Address to the Synod of Bishops', *Zenit*, 11 October 2012, https://zenit.org/2012/10/11/archbishop-rowan-williams-address-to-the-synod-of-bishops/, accessed 19.03.2025.

[3] Smiljanic, *Our Thoughts Determine Our Lives*, p. 66.

41

AN ECOLOGY OF LOVE

'Music and silence – how I detest them both!' exclaims C. S. Lewis's character Screwtape, a senior devil who has mastered the arts of both temptation and manipulation. All that resembles heaven, he explains to his nephew Wormwood, should be replaced with noise, 'which alone defends us from silly qualms, despairing scruples, and impossible desires.' No doubt Screwtape would approve of social media and the constant barrage of the marketing industry. Noise distracts our attention from what is most important, precious and good.

How we perceive reality is intimately bound up with the faculty of attention. To paraphrase William James, philosopher and pioneer of modern psychology, in the moment of attention, what we attend to *is* reality.[1] What we overlook or ignore falls outside the world of our concern. What we don't give attention to becomes less real, unimportant, regardless of how real and important it may be. In a very real sense, we choose the world we inhabit through what we give attention to and by the quality of our attention, though for many of us our 'choices' go unnoticed. Driven by conditioning and habits of which we are largely unaware, our choices are mostly unconscious, and so are barely our choices at all.

Whether we have the technological and financial resources needed to halt the tragedy of human-caused climate change and ecological destruction isn't in question. What *is* in question is the extent to

---

[1] William James, *The Principles of Psychology* (New York: Dover Publications, 1958), II: p. 322.

which hearts can be awakened, whether governments and corporates can move from a mindset of self-oriented competition to conscious, ecologically-aware collaboration. One way or another, we have created a way of seeing, a way of being, which is dislocated and dislocating, which encourages us to forget that every atom of our body, every breath we inhale, is pure gift. But it doesn't have to be like this. We can wake up. We can choose a new way of seeing, a new way of being.

Truly great books for children convey great truths for all of us. Margery Williams' classic book *The Velveteen Rabbit* tells us something of singular importance for our relationship with the world. 'Real isn't how you are made', the Skin Horse tells the Rabbit, 'It's something that happens to you. When a child loves you for a long, long time, not just to play with, but really loves you, then you become Real.'[2] When the Pulitzer Prize-winning writer and environmental activist Gary Snyder was once asked if he had any advice about climate change and the ecological crisis, he replied, 'Don't feel guilty. Guilt and anger and fear are part of the problem. If you want to save the world, save it because you love it!'[3] We can only love – and will only want to save – what is *real* to us. And things become real for us in the light of loving attention.

It's crucial that we find ways to challenge the narratives and cultural forces that encourage us to see ourselves as separate from the world. But it's not enough to simply understand non-separateness as a rational, attractive-sounding proposition. To bring about real, lasting change, we need to touch the truth of non-separateness, to know it for ourselves. The invitation of meditation is to discover that the deepest truth of who we are is the deepest truth of everything, to come home to the simple reality of life, unmediated by our stories about it. We are invited to deep communion. We do not come to this by a process of thought or analysis (though thought and analysis can help clear the path). We come to the truth of non-separateness, of

---

[2] Margery Williams, *The Velveteen Rabbit* (New York: George H. Doran, 1922), pp. 5–8.

[3] Cited in Jack Kornfield, *No Time Like the Present: Finding Freedom, Love and Joy Right Where you Are* (London: Penguin Random House, 2017), p. 213.

oneness, through the practice of loving attention, through clearing a space for encounter.

The revolution that's so badly needed begins within each of us. Everything we need to find a new way of living is waiting within our hearts. With the energy of loving attention we can cultivate a new relationship with the Earth and all her inhabitants. 'The mystery of God in Christ', writes Martin Laird,

> seeks to bring Himself to others *through* us, as food for the hungry, clothing for the naked, justice for the imprisoned, and compassion for the stranger, the widow, and the orphan. Contemplation, and the lifestyle flowing from it, asks but a single question, 'What does kindness look like at any given moment?'[4]

---

[4] Martin Laird, *An Ocean of Light: Contemplation, Transformation and Liberation* (Oxford: Oxford University Press, 2019), p. 16 (emphasis added).

42

PRESENT-WITH, PRESENT-FOR

The fruits of meditation manifest in every aspect of our lives, but supremely in our relationships. It is vital that we understand this and don't imagine that the so-called 'spiritual life' is somehow separate from the fullness of our ordinary life, lived together. All that we are, all that we have, is born in and through *relationship*.

There are many ways in which our silent practice helps us in our relationships with others. One important way is that in learning to be present with God, without wanting to do anything or receive anything, we learn to be simply *present-with* and *present-for* those around us. It is very understandable that we want to help those around us and alleviate their suffering. There is so much that needs to be done. But sometimes our strong desire to make a difference, to be of use, can be a hindrance. Our own ideas and plans can cloud our minds and make us less capable of listening. We can miss what others might really need from us.

In meditation, Christ guides us into the quiet spaciousness of God's love, so we can become ourselves. And as we become ourselves, we increasingly share the love we receive by allowing space for others to be themselves. We allow God to love *through* us. We become places where the kingdom *happens*. The Dominican theologian Herbert McCabe wrote wonderfully about the spacious letting-be of love:

> What you give someone when you give them love is the gift of yourself. And what does that mean? It means you give them space. You give them a place where they can be

themselves. To give someone love is to give her herself, to give him himself, to let him be. What gives us elbow room, what gives us space to grow and become ourselves, is the love that comes to us from another. Love is a space in which to expand, and it is always a gift. In this sense we receive ourselves from the hands of others.

Of course, this is true in innumerable ways – we have to be born of others, for a start – but our growth, our personal development, also takes place in the space that others provide by their love. It is a space we cannot just take for granted but which, in another sense, we can only take for granted to us by someone who loves us. To give love is to give the precious space of nothing, space. To give love is to let be. The power of God is pre-eminently the power to let things be.[1]

In meditation we learn to be present with God without wanting to receive anything or do anything. We learn to be present with those around us in simple solidarity, however their life is for them at that moment.

---

[1] Herbert McCabe, *God Matters* (London: Bloomsbury Publishing, 2006), p. 108.

43

'BLESSED ARE THE PEACEMAKERS'

The origins of words may not always strike us as especially interesting or important. But sometimes they are both, and 'religion' is a good example. It is especially important to remember some of the deepest meanings of this word at moments when some may wish to use it as a way of dividing people. While the origins of the word 'religion' are not entirely clear, it appears to come from combining the Latin *re*, meaning 'again' or 'back', and *ligio*, meaning 'to connect' or 'tie' or 'bind together'. Far from being something to be used to divide people, 'religion' means 'a way of getting back in touch', something that 'reconnects' and 'binds together'. With this deeper meaning in mind, we might also say that to be unaware of or to reject the contemplative dimension of religion, is to be unaware of or to reject the purpose of religion. Contemplation – the gift of seeing clearly, which the practice of meditation helps open us to receive – is all about getting back in touch, reconnecting with that which binds us together.

The contemplative dimension is the heart of every religion, helping us come to awareness of our essential oneness with each other and all creation in the oneness of God. The great wisdom teachings of the Old and New Testaments, as well as the wisdom teachings of the Koran, of the Vedas and Upanishads, of the Buddhist Sutras and the great ancestral religions of Australia and the Americas (to name but a few), all bear witness to the truth of oneness, and our need to manifest (incarnate) this truth in our relationships, through our care of each other, through our care of the whole of creation. The two are not separate. Religion: a way of getting back in touch, of reconnecting, of binding together. As Sister Wendy Beckett writes, 'Think of religion as a trellis, a framework, on which the vine of love can grow.'[1] Meditation: a simple practice which opens to receive the gift of contemplation, the gift of seeing clearly and living the truth of oneness. May they be one, Jesus prayed, 'may they be brought to completion as one' (John 17.22–23).

Speaking as a Christian, I like to imagine the extraordinary difference that Christians might make in bringing about greater peace in the world if they were to embrace the contemplative dimension of the Gospel. We have been given all we need for a new understanding of ourselves and of each other, as not separate, but one. We have been given all we need to come home to the mystery of God's presence within all creation, and to manifest this presence in the practice of unselfish love. We have all been given all that we need for a new way of seeing and a new way of being. The heartbreaking conflicts in our world make us painfully aware of the need for peace in the world, of the need to do what we can (however modest) to help create a better future for all.

The Sermon on the Mount is understood by many to be a record of Jesus' essential teaching, and it begins with what are known as the Beatitudes (Matt. 5.3–11). The Beatitudes are not commandments, not a list of things we need to do (or not do). They tell us what we will see if we look at certain people in certain situations. They are descriptions of a way of being which we might call 'blessedness' or 'holiness', in the sense that this is what it looks like to be whole, to be one.

Many of us might look at the Beatitudes and feel slightly nervous. We might say to ourselves, 'I'll never be able to live like this! They must surely be meant for others.' But the seeds of the Beatitudes are in all of us. They are part and parcel of who we are. We just need to become aware of these seeds, and decide to water them and tend to them. God takes care of the rest. Ultimately, the Beatitudes are one. As the different colours refracted by a prism are never other than the single source of light, the Beatitudes are expressions of a single love. This is what it looks like to be fully, radically human, to be *one*.

---

[1] Sister Wendy Beckett, *Sister Wendy on Prayer* (London: Bloomsbury, 2006), p. 69.

Our lives can become the radiance of divine love, because God, love, is the deepest truth of who we are. Meditation is a simple way of saying 'Yes' to God bringing this about, that we might manifest in our bodies the divine truth of who we are, shining in and through our relationships.

If we want to help bring more peace into the world, the work always begins right *here*, right *now*. We have each been given all that we need for a new way of seeing and a new way of being. Each of us can contribute to peace in the world through watering and tending to the seeds of peace within ourselves.

Blessed are the peacemakers; they shall be called the radiance of divine love

Blessed are those whose presence is an open hand, held out from an open heart, a quiet bridge to our common home.

Blessed are those who bring the gift of silence to the noise of anger and conflict.

Blessed are those who have surrendered the need for control, who allow the Spirit of peace to breathe through them without resistance, and so become the breath of peace for others.

Blessed are those who can listen patiently in the absence of easy answers, who can wait patiently in the darkness of not-knowing.

Blessed are those who gently silence the accusing and judgemental voices by means of their silence.

Blessed are those whose tears of self-acceptance have transformed their fear and anger into the energy of reconciliation.

Blessed are those who have allowed their suffering to become a womb of compassion for others, whose pain has given birth to unconditional love.

Blessed are those whose openness provides a space for all voices on the shared journey of becoming who we are.

Blessed are those who have become so self-forgetful that they no longer have anything to defend, who have lost themselves in God and become like windows of light.

THE SCHOOL OF CONTEMPLATIVE LIFE

*Once we've found such peace
within, it spreads light and joy
to gift peace without.*

An invitation to you

Dear Reader,

The School of Contemplative Life teaches meditation from the Christian wisdom tradition as a spiritual path to peace, community and oneness – as a way of clearing space to encounter the divine nature of life.

At the heart of our work is an online practice community. We host free, twice-weekly gatherings providing a supportive space where people can learn to meditate, practice together, and gain an appreciation of contemplative Christianity through teachings which draw on a wide range of voices from across the centuries.

Whatever your background, beliefs, or experience of meditation, you are most welcome to join us. Walking this liberating path is so much easier and more joyful when we are supported and encouraged by the presence of others.

For more information about our online practice community, as well as our in-person and online retreats, please visit our website, www.schoolofcontemplativelife.com. Everyone is welcome.

All peace,
Chris Whittington
Founder of The School of Contemplative Life

About The School of Contemplative Life

The seed that germinated into The School of Contemplative Life was quietly planted when, aged 19, I arrived at Prinknash Abbey Benedictine Monastery and began several years of formation under the monks' wise and gentle guidance.

Fast-forward to the Covid-19 pandemic and our offering a series of peace-themed online meditation workshops during the months when people were asked to avoid social contact and remain at home. Much to our surprise, over 2,000 people attended the workshops, including schoolteachers and church leaders, healthcare workers and stay-at-home parents, retired individuals, university students and business professionals, people of all faiths and none. The breadth of interest surprised us, together with the outpouring of stories people shared about the deep impact the practice was having in their lives – such as the words below –

> The simple practice of silent meditation is profound. I do not begin to understand how it is proving to have such a positive effect on my relationships. I feel more at one with others and with the Spirit than I have ever experienced before. I and my colleagues have discovered a simple pathway to mental peace. (Headteacher)

Our hope for the School is the same hope that inspired this little book: to help people discover an ancient jewel within the riches of a contemplative tradition which might be described as the missing piece of much contemporary Christianity.

Our aims are:

- To contribute to the restoration of contemplative practice as a way of life which purifies our motives and opens us to the Divine – the foundation of peace within us and between us, the deepest basis for our care of each other and our precious world.
- To promote the inseparable relationship between interior transformation and social transformation.
- To be a source of peace and an antidote to the fundamentalism which gives rise to so much conflict and violence in the world.

- To nurture the common ground between religions by teaching meditation from the Christian wisdom tradition as a simple, universal practice for all people.

Scan the QR code below to sign up to our free online meditation.

www.ingramcontent.com/pod-product-compliance
Lightning Source LLC
Chambersburg PA
CBHW060612080526
44585CB00013B/792